CW01306829

What Every Parent and Teacher Should Know:
Real Life Stories by a Senior Educationalist.

by

Roy J Andersen

The Moving Quill Publishing House

MQ

Copyright © Roy Andersen. 2013

The right of Roy Andersen to be identified as the author of this work has been asserted by him in accordance with the Copyright Designs and Patents Act 1988. All rights reserved. No part of this publication may be reproduced, stored in a retrieval system, or transmitted, in any form or by any means, electronic, mechanical, photocopying, recording, or otherwise, without the prior written permission of the copyright owner.

Disclaimer:
The author and the publisher will assume no liability nor responsibility to any person or entity with respect to any loss or damage related directly or indirectly to the information in this book. Neither the author nor the publisher will provide any remedy for indirect, consequential, punitive, or incidental damages arising from this book, including such from negligence, strict liability, or breach of warranty or contract, even after notice of the possibility of such damages. Neither the publisher nor the author accept any responsibility for the actions of another based on the information in this book.

ISBN: 9798343268065

Table of Contents

Introduction   3

Chapter One: 12
    Thomas

Chapter Two: 15
The School Life

Chapter Three: 39
    The Mother

Chapter Four: 62
    The Son

Chapter Five: 76
    Mathew

Chapter Six: 83
    "Why Did They Say That About My Son?"

Chapter Seven: 108
    I Meet the Parents

Chapter Eight: 143
    Paul

Chapter Nine: 147
    How to Help Students Get Better Grades

Chapter Ten: 176
    18-Month-Old Lizzy

Chapter Eleven: Chris and Little Bell	183
Chapter Twelve: The Bullied Child	188
Chapter Thirteen: A Class in Learning	197

Chapter Fourteen:
    Times of Artificial Intelligence:
        Not what you think
	213

Further books by Roy Andersen	236
Online Teacher Training Course	255
References	262

Foreword

It is with pride and professional pleasure that I write this Foreword for a pioneering book authored by Roy Andersen. Today in the field of education, we are finally beginning once again (after a period of almost 50 years) to recognise the vital importance of cognitive development in our children.

This cognitive development is, for most individuals, a process that does not happen sufficiently in itself; it requires explicit activity on the part of parents, teachers, caregivers, and others. While we know that it's possible to acquire cognitive strategies in later life, it is never too late to improve one's thinking patterns, at the same time, early development by parents is essential whenever possible.

Even though most parents of young children today were not the beneficiaries themselves of systematic cognitive education in their own schooling, nonetheless it is not only possible but also necessary that they provide that foundation in thinking skills for their children, at an early age if possible.

Some will say that this development is the responsibility of the school, and of course, the school's role is of critical importance. However, we must remember that a school-age child may spend 40 hours or less per week in formal schooling (less in a number of countries), while there are 168 hours in the week (some of which, of course, should be spent in sleep). And formal schooling does not begin until after the development of some essential brain-patterning which can occur within the first two years of life.

This simple statistical comparison indicates that parents have the potential for at least as much, and perhaps more in some ways influence on their children's development as does the school. This important book designed as much for parents, as for teachers, indicates the rationale and process for how both can enhance the child's thinking process.

Clearly, the most powerful combination of forces would be the home and the school working together; helping schools to understand and implement the process of cognitive education for their part is the subject of other writings by Roy Andersen. With this book in hand, however, interested and dedicated parents can gain important understandings as well as procedures for their part in enabling tomorrow's adults to reach their fullest possible cognitive potential while there is still time to do so.

Prof. David Martin. PhD
Dean Emeritus Gallaudet University, Washington D.C.

About Me

I did not do well in school. In fact, I failed every one of my final examinations and left school virtually illiterate. Yet, four years later, I was to pass all of these examinations and those considerably far, far higher with the highest distinction.

This achievement seeded in me a quest to understand not just what was and still is wrong with the school system, but also how children learn and what stops them from learning better. As I sought to improve the ways children could learn, I worked as a teacher through all the levels of education from kindergarten, through primary and secondary school and then in university.

For 45 years, I have struggled to share the thoughts and insights I gained with other teachers and parents in how children could learn better. Eventually, I was to devise not only a new method of teaching but also a new understanding of what intelligence could be. It was inevitable from this background that I should become a consultant to help students of any age to better understand not just what they were learning, but how they could learn the skill of what we call intelligence.

As my experience in this developed, I was able to explain to my students the processes their mind and brain go through to understand their world, and the skills they can develop to explain their mind better to others to achieve far higher recognition. The classes I worked with improved in their overall performance and the individuals I helped gained far higher grades. This book tells a little of some of the wonderful human beings I have met, and what I learned from them.

Roy Andersen 2024

* * *

What the Experts say:

"It will probably take a few years, possibly even a decade before the public at large will get how revolutionary the ideas of Roy Andersen are.

His ideas resonate perfectly with the Learnable Theory and are destined to impact not only teaching in schools, but also the way human resources are selected and developed in organisations. Indeed, Roy's deconstruction of intelligence goes well beyond Daniel Coleman, Howard Gardner and what others have done so far. Roy goes at the root of learning, he links it to the creation and leveraging of meanings and how the symbolic process of language plays a key role in what we generally identify and name intelligence.

It is for these reasons that I am inclined to believe that Roy's ideas have the potential to promote a major turn around in multiple educational fields and practices, including Managerial Sciences."

Professor Luca Magni. LUISS Business School. Rome. Italy

"What Every Parent and Teacher Should Know' is written by a teacher who teaches from the heart. Every school should put this book in the hands of all school staff. School leaders should provide opportunities for weekly dialogue. These conversations can build teacher and student capacity toward teaching and learning."

Dr Gwendolyn Lavert. Educational Consultant. U.S.A.

"Roy's series of books clearly and methodically maps out exactly how students learn. He isn't afraid to address head-on the many mis-conceptions that are plaguing our society and thus having a negative impact on our students' learning. Parents and educators who read these books will not only have a better understanding, but will also be inspired to change in their attitudes and preconceived notions on how students can excel in their learning.

If you've ever wanted to unravel how students learn, then these books are the answer you have been looking for! They should be mandatory reading for every parent and educator."

Erin Calhoun. National Institute of Learning Development. USA

"The most important books I have ever read about a child's intelligence."

Prof. Tatyana Oleinik. Pedagogical University. Ukraine.

"*What Every Parent and Teacher Should Know* appears to me to be very relevant to those currently teaching and particularly those who are just starting their career. Whilst presented as stories, they contextualise the learning process and provide clear and well developed scenarios and ideas of problems faced by learners, reasons for them and importantly how teachers can start to address the different challenges they and their learners face in the mainstream classroom. In short, I think the book would make a great addition to any initial teacher training reading list."

Ian Arkell. Educational Consultant CEO SchoolPro. UK

"Roy's books should be read by every parent and educator in the world. They do represent a real breakthrough in our understanding of what intelligence is and how it develops, and the importance of changing the ways students are both parented and educated. Roy is doing for learning the work that is as significant as was that done in the past by such figures as John Dewey. These are must-reads for both parents and educators alike."

Dean Emeritus David Martin PhD Gallaudet University / Prof Washington, D.C. USA.

"The whole set of Roy's books should be in the library of each school in every corner of the world. They should also be part of the syllabus in the institutions who are offering child psychology, and teacher training diplomas and degree programs, or at least they should be the part of a refresher course."

M.Imran Khan. CEO AIMMS Universities. Middle East

"These are very important and interesting books, with lots of valuable points for parents and teachers. They bring learning and education to a whole new level. Well done!"

Prof. Mads Hermansen. Educational Psychologist Denmark.

You can see more of the books I have written and more testimonials at

www.andersenroy.com

*The greatest adventure is not in exploring new lands,
it is seeing through new eyes.*

By
John the Brush

John is a professional cartoonist of considerable distinction and international merit. He really loves his job, and I know would be delighted to hear from anyone seeking assistance with a cartoon.

John can be contacted at: smiggysmyth@gmail.com

The Construction of School
and
The Secret of How it Works

Learning in school is not rocket science. Any child born with normal mental ability, as the very most are, can gain the highest marks in a class and top grades in any examination if, and only if, they keep up with the steady build up of rules upon which the information of school works.

School learning is gained through a never ending series of rules. Rules to define when to sit and when to move, to teach the child how to keep order in the class so they behave and concentrate in their lessons. Rules in mathematics to know how to transpose numbers about. Rules in grammar to know how to spell words, create sentences and construct a story so the child can compose an answer efficiently.

Rules to create memory networks to recall facts to be learnt. If the child/student pays attention and learns and practices each rule they are presented with, they understand how to think when negotiating through a learning task and feel confident to apply their learning to other areas and develop critical thinking through their confidence and curiosity.

However, should they miss a rule, which the very, very most do, because they were distracted by some concern or more attracted by another thought or bored, they do not know how to move correctly through a learning task. Fearful of being laughed at for asking the teacher for help or unable to gain a satisfactory understanding from the teacher if they did ask, they guess how to proceed. Invariably, they guess wrongly and move into a series of errors not understanding why they are wrong. The lesser mark they gain from the teacher for their effort disillusions them and they lose confidence to believe they can master the subject which leads to disinterest then lack of effort.

Rules come in many forms. A very simple example would be the rule to create a question from the word "there." The question is made by adding "w" before the "t", to create the word "where." However, if the child does not learn this rule, they can confuse usage with the past tense of are, which is "were." So, they write "were where we?" instead of "where were we?" and lose a mark. Each mark lost, moves them further down from being the top of the class. School performance, albeit ability, is only about keeping up with the rules.

Therefore, each student in a class is evaluated on the marks they gain, which is derived from the marks they lost. The more rules the child/student missed or misunderstood, so the lower their score will be when compared with others in the class.

Over time each student will build up a profile of their worth by the rules they have understood or missed, which will give them a standing in the class.

For those who kept up with all or most of the rules, they will score the most and be top of the class. For those who missed most rules, they will be the most confused in their learning, score the least and be bottom of the class. The rest of the class will lie between these two extremes, being more or less confused by the rules they have misunderstood, not learnt and not practiced against those they did learn and became competent with.

Yet, teachers too little explain this to their students. Students simply get a mark, high, low or average and don't know why or what they could do to otherwise improve. They simply believe the worth the teacher gives them, and too often role play to this.

So, evaluation is made of how each student as they progress in their learning. How well the student is able to present the facts to be known and how well they have learnt the relevant rules to tell 'their story' will much be decided by the quality of language they were raised in or since developed. Their competence in language, whether this be the language used in the school for communication such as English, Chinese or Arabic and the language of mathematics, will much determine how they rate in any evaluation.

Since the classroom has a competitive atmosphere, students strive against each other, affecting the egos, drives and sense of security of each. The best student will strive to remain to be the best and put in the effort to beat any competition. The worst student will not understand what they are not doing right and will have no confidence in their teacher, their class or themselves. They will tend to disrupt the learning of the class to gain some level of acknowledgement to their presence. The students between these extremes will struggle constantly against each other seeking to obtain less red scribbles and a higher mark each time their work is appraised.

As the best in the class will be regarded to be the smartest and then the most intelligent, so the worst will be regarded as least intelligent with lack of interest. The rest of the class will be thought of as trying as much as they are able. This "as much" means their natural ability plus their effort.

This distinction between ability and effort being genuinely confused by teachers just as by psychologists, since nobody truly understands what a genetic value of intelligence means. However, the term genetic competence that was openly discussed in the past is scarily mentioned today, since all children must be seen to be given equal and fair opportunity in education. Yet, this factor lingers in the back of a teacher's mind.

Yet, consideration of the student's intelligence here is very wrong. The degree of intelligence of a student, whatever this may be thought to be, plays no role in their understanding of a rule and their effort to be competent with the rule, since all rules are very simple to understand and build up with a steadily regularity.

It is only when a student loses track with the build up of these rules, which they can do for a large number of reasons, that they become confused in how to think because they miss the tools that enable them to do this.

With diminishing confidence they hold themselves back from interacting boldly, fearful of ridicule in the class. As they interact less, they have less opportunity to test what they think they have learnt and fail to understand ever more.

As years pass, each student gains a certain profile which is judged to decide if they will move to the university level or not. It is important to know now that school does not teach children how to think or how to reason. There is a purpose to this, which we unveil in our book "Intelligence: The Great Lie".

The student's competence in reasoning comes from their home background and the individuals they spent short time with who gave them guidance in this. There is no specific subject for this, as there should be, but there again there is a purpose for this. The students who move to the university level are taught how to reason and how to think better, because there are to be the future managers in society and industry who will be take more responsible roles in their society and are to be prepared for this.

The students who have not learnt the rules satisfactorily through their many years of school, will be thought to lack the necessary self responsibility required for managerial roles in society and not be forwarded to university. Deprived of the higher education in their reason, they will move from school to work or some simpler education preparing them for this, where they will become the citizen worker in the society required to follow and not too much contest the guidance of their managers.

This is school and this is how it works!

Roy Andersen

What Every Parent and Teacher Should Know:

Real Life Stories by a Senior Educationalist.

Introduction

OFSTED is an acronym for The Office for Standards in Education, Children's Services and Skills. It is a government organisation responsible for inspecting the standard of schools in the UK. The high school in my village was awarded full marks by OFSTED not too long ago, and so prompted as being one of the best schools in the UK. The school proudly displays its achievement outside the main gates, and the reception hall is littered with OFSTED remarks and posters. It is an advertisement for the achievement of this school, as much as it is for recognition of the work that OFSTED does. It was, then, very interesting for me to talk to a former student of this school, while I waited for a bus.

"I'm glad to see you here," I remarked as I arrived panting at the bus stop near the school, "thought the bus might have passed."

"No. It's always late," he replied.

We talked about one or two things, and then looking at him I asked,

"Are you a student at the school?"

"I was, but now I'm at Art College."

"Don't mind me asking, but when did you leave the school?"

"Oh, two years ago." He was nonchalant in his reply.

Now! Two years ago was when OFSTED made their investigation and award to this school. So, it was very interesting for me to know of his personal experiences there at this time.

"So, tell me," I asked, "what did you think of the teachers?'

"Some were OK," he said in a matter-of-fact manner.

"How did you feel about their teaching? Did you feel they knew a lot about what they were teaching?"

He half laughed to himself. "Some did," he told me, "but others did not seem to know too much. Some students knew more than the teachers. They would just tell us to work from textbooks or give PowerPoint presentations. But! Nothing really made much sense. I mean, it was boring just to sit in the class, and be shown slides and told points to remember.

Anyway, lessons were always boring, because we never learned anything interesting. Everything was just about how to answer exam questions. Lessons were only about the types of questions we could be asked, and the best way to answer them. There was never any interest as to why we should learn the subject, just to pass exams often," he continued, "I did not understand what I was doing, and if I asked the teacher they didn't really explain it to me. We were, more or less, left to make our own sense of what was in the textbook. So, we kind of relied upon one or two in the class to tell us the answers in the break or after school."

Nothing has changed, I thought to myself. It was the same when I was at school. I remembered then reading a letter that a 16-year-old girl had recently written in America.

"I can go weeks in most of my classes," she wrote, "without doing homework and still maintain a grade of 'B'. The curriculum is not challenging so no one is trying. Teachers don't care, and people constantly say we can't do it. So we no longer try."[i]

Moving to another thought, I mentioned to my new friend, "You know, the big thing now is to look for any student who does not keep up with the rest and suspect them of dyslexia."

"Tell me about it," he said. "Mind you, we look forward to being told we are because then we get extra help in the lesson by an assistant teacher to understand what is going on. But the big thing is that we get an extra 25 minutes in an exam. This really makes a big difference."

"Are you dyslexic?" I asked him.

"Well, I went to the teacher in my last year and asked her. They gave me some tests and said I had a small learning problem. The first time in my whole life anyone has said this to me and this in the very last year. So, I was really glad they said this. It gave me the time I needed in my exams to get a better grade." (And for the school in the league table, I thought.)

"Tell me," I asked him, changing the subject, "was there a lot of bullying going on?"

"It was quite common. Not for me, but I know how it affected others in my class." His reply was not totally convincing.

"How did the teachers keep control, if things got out of order? In my days they used to just cane us," I told him,

"I know some teachers want to bring it back."

"I don't think it made a big difference then. It was just a fact of life. I remember they told me when I was in school that I was too stupid for languages, so I was put in for rural studies." He was not familiar with this, so I explained, "It's about teaching the value of nature. I never understood what that meant because I can only remember being taken on nature walks.

So, on the last lesson of every Friday morning, Old Tom with a walking stick, an elderly teacher (God knows how teachers working in their late seventies will ever manage), would take us outside. Now, there was a high brick wall surrounding the school with one door at the back that led to the fields. At the appointed time, Tom would unlock the door and usher us through it in an orderly line. But once the last boy was out, we broke ranks and ran anywhere we wanted.

Old Tom would chase us, but he could never catch up. We would run to a deep ditch, walk over a large pipe that spanned it, and then we were free. He never attempted to try and would shout and wave his stick while we climbed trees and swung about on ropes. After a while, Old Tom would give up, and we would laugh and have fun. But the thing was that then we would realise it was lunchtime, and amble back to the back door in the wall.

Every Friday, the same thing happened. Old Tom would take us out, we would escape, return to the door (it was the only way back in) and he would be waiting behind it. As each opened the door, a hand would come down from behind it and grab him by the collar. The whole class would have to line up, bend over and each of us got six of the best. Then, we went to lunch, and so to the next Friday. We just took caning as a thing that happened normally. It hurt a bit for half an hour, but it was soon forgotten. It was far, far more important to escape!"

He looked at me as if he could never imagine having a school time like that. There never was an escape for him. "Well, we just got a yellow or a red slip," he told me.

"Tell me about these slips?" I asked him.

"Well, you'd get a yellow slip if you forgot your homework, or didn't do it," He smiled. "Two yellows meant a red, and a red was given out for bad behaviour. Once you got a red, you were put in detention."

"That sounds a little ominous. What happened in detention?"
"Oh! Not much. We just had to stay behind a bit, and do our homework in the class," he told me in a disinterested manner.

"Did you think the class was well behaved?"

"Sometimes," Then a smile slowly came to his face. "Sometimes, the teacher would just walk out. I mean, they completely left the classroom when we got out of hand."

"You mean there was no teacher there! The class was just abandoned?" I could feel the shock in my voice as I said this.

He smiled again. He knew I understood what he meant.

"But this school got the highest OFSTED award," I reminded him and then wondered what incentives and bribes had been passed 'under the table' to prevent teachers fleeing their classroom and students made to look impeccably well behaved for the whole of the two-day inspection.

"Well, many passed exams, so we got a good score for the school. But we didn't learn anything. Besides," he added, "the primary school in the village failed OFSTED that year, so I suppose they had to make one school look good."

It's all politics, I thought to myself, as I remembered the words of a teacher who has been teaching for 20 years.

"School today," she told me when we met last year, "is not now about teaching students how to gain knowledge as it should be. It's about teaching them to pass exams, and so how the school comes out in performance ratings. Many head-teachers are not really interested in their school or their students; it's just about how efficient they can make the school look as they look for the next step on the career ladder."

I have seen this myself and heard from other quarters of the damaging effect of making schools competitive with each other. It has created a huge business machine where the only thought is for each school to get the most of their students through exams with the highest grades.

On the outset, it may have seemed a good idea, but since the school staff can be just as ingenious when seeking to prove they belong to a better school (which improves their career prospects), as their students can be to avoid learning, lessons soon took the form of exam strategies. No longer were students to be guided in why and how their subject came about or the applications of it to real life (which is what learning must become in this century if we are to create citizens more able and adaptable in their thinking), instead, they are to be drilled on previous exam questions and taught aspects that are most likely to come up in examinations.

Jeremy Clarkson of Top Gear fame beautifully illustrated the effect and the travesty of league tables, when he explained how a girl insisted on taking three science subjects for her A levels. Her head-teacher strongly tried to dissuade her, suggesting she should take subjects she could get high passes in, such as cookery! However, the girl persisted (perhaps because she had a career in mind), sat the science exams, and scored one C and two Ds, which made her dream possible, however, only just. As a direct result of this, her school dropped fifty places in the league table.[1] I have heard such comments as these from educationalists in many countries.

In truth, we have lost the purpose of what school is meant to be, because now students seldom understand why they are learning a subject or of the greater meaning to this in their life. No wonder that too many leave school with no clue as to what they would like to do with their life, as my art college friend explained to me. After all, when students are raised to focus only on examinations, they are deprived of the essence that drives their interest and this which awakens their fascination. It is this drive that sets their mind off to experience and to learn.

Is it then so surprising that without such interest, 57% of American students questioned did not know the dates of their Civil War to within half a century,[2] even though their national identity is founded upon this? Another study found that 72% of American students tested did not know that America fought Hitler in WW2.[3] We may equally point out that 36% of a sample of British students, between the ages of 16 to 23, did not know that bacon comes from pigs, and 40% did not know that milk comes from cows. In fact, 7% thought that milk actually comes from wheat.[4]

Teachers are leaving education in their droves, at least those young enough to do so. Others try to hold out until retirement. In 2015, 40% of new teachers quit within the first 12 months of starting work. Teaching is not what they had imagined it to be. Since this exodus is a global phenomenon at a time when the student population is increasing, we must face the all too obvious danger of computers taking over the education process.

Many people think that computer learning means that each student can learn at their own pace. The reality is that computers do not raise the awareness or the intelligence of students. Go into any shop and ask the ex-student newly employed an arithmetic question about the money you have just given them. Ten to one their mind will be blank until they push the button of a little machine that will tell them the answer. Mental arithmetic is not just about counting money, it's a good indication as to how aware you are of the world about you, in other words, real-life intelligence.

Yet, what is not discussed, at least I have not met anyone who does, is the real social danger of computerised education. Children, who learn to think through an android, do not develop well the skills of being human. A computer gives no sense of humanness when you give the wrong answer. If its program tries to do so, it is only to excite you to the next level. By raising our children on too much computer time in education, we risk the danger of creating future generations who are not aware of the values of compassion and empathy that inspire us to be human, at a time when their work and the social world will be totally under the influence of artificial intelligence.

Teaching is not easy today, but we owe it to ourselves to try to create a generation of more adaptable intelligence and greater social empathy than we were raised to have so that our children of today stand a better chance of living their lives in peace and greater harmony.

It is for all the reasons I have mentioned in this introduction, that I want to explain to you why I love to be a teacher, and why I want to share the joy and meanings I have gained in opening doors of imagination and purpose to so many children, as I came to realise just what learning means.

Chapter One
Thomas

I had to help a child who had fallen over and grazed their knee and found myself running a little late for my new class. I wondered, as I turned tears into a smile, how many other teachers always carry a few spare plasters with them. As I walked along the now empty corridor, and with no sound coming from beyond the closed door of each classroom I passed, it was almost as if the school was deserted. This, however, was an illusion shortly to be shattered.

I had turned the handle and barely opened the door to my classroom, when I was greeted with the sound of a girl's scream. A boy ran in front of me chased by another, and I watched, mesmerised for a moment, as a paper aeroplane sailed through the air before hitting a light shade and then crash-dive to the floor. Here we go again, I thought.

The thing is that if you want to teach kids you have to stop being an adult, well, at least on the surface. So, while few had noticed I had entered the room, and instead of shouting to try to bring order, I became a pied piper to my little class.

Pretending I was playing the trumpet, I at fifty years of age began to dance merrily up the aisle between the desks, not taking notice of anyone, but aware of a boy who had quickly realized this could be a great game and had come behind me playing his invisible drum. This caught on like wildfire. Kids, who moments before were running, laughing, crying, shouting in an unimaginable frenzy, were now following me in line around the desks, chairs, fields, meadows, streams, and hamlets of their minds. I had noticed from entering the room, one boy who was happily sitting under his desk.

As I brought 'my troops' back to their desks, I tried to encourage this child to come out from under his, but he only grinned back and remained firmly where he was. I knew not to try to ease him out. He would have resisted or only moved under another desk or shot back here the moment I released him. This was his game. He had resisted longer than others in his class the transition from free childhood to the civilised conformity that would be required of him by the school.

He was delighted when I let him stay where he was, while I addressed the rest of the class. He laughed out loud when I looked down at him, pretending that I had forgotten where he was. There is usually such a character in a class, the clown who plays to attention. But instead of shouting at him, I played along. I asked all the students to join me, as I crawled under a desk and sat near him.

"Now," I told them, "let's begin the lesson," and so this is how we started, all sitting under desks, all happy and none feeling restricted. As the time of the lesson moved, I pretended to show them how painful it was for my back to sit like this, so I moved to sit against the wall. The children joined and sat around me, except that is for my little friend.

So, I played a game with him until he eventually decided to crawl out from where he was and sit with the group. As I carried on with the lesson, I found that he had moved closer to me and after sometime came to lay his head on my legs. This was just love, and what he needed.

The next lesson was also held on the floor and the one after that. It took me about a month to get all, and I mean all, sitting behind their desks in the lesson. On the fifth week, I opened the door and there was my star pupil sitting on his chair, behind his desk with a huge grin on his face. Thomas turned out to be the pupil who asked me the most questions in a lesson, and who earned the highest marks as the year came to an end.

Other teachers I found had screamed and shouted at this class. It was not my way. The problem with teachers who shout is that they demand the child behaves like an adult. If you want to teach children, you have to go into their magical world where the only rule is fun.

To pull them into our world they just need their space, a teacher they can feel is one of them, and a personality they can identify with and trust. Plus, I may add, a bag of sweets! Sweets, I learned a long time ago, will take the teacher places shouting never could, and with the right approach, they are as successful with undergraduates as they are with those in grade 1. Learning then did not have to be sitting rigid behind a desk. All I wanted with these eight-year-olds was their attention to reveal a beautiful story of why a Chinese emperor once decreed that a noun should never lead an article.

Chapter Two
The School Life

The teacher was kind, the children looked happy. The lesson had begun, and by now each was examining the textbook before them or scribbling their thoughts into their exercise book. Some seemed to know what to do. Others did not. As always, one child passed a piece of paper to another when the teacher was not looking, and one sneered at another. Gossip and rivalry, like father, like son I thought, as they would most likely behave later in life. Friends whispered, and one was texting with their mobile phone hidden, or so they thought, under their desk. The teacher walked around, looking over the shoulders of each as she passed them.

I had been asked to join the lesson by the vice principal of Laura's acquaintance. We shall meet Laura later in our story. The vice principal was a kind man. Older than the other teachers I had met in this school and well versed in the ways of the world. A retired sea captain I was told, although he did not look the part. He was neither a fat, jovial man nor did he wear a stern-looking beard. He was just, well, normal looking. I could have imagined him more to be a retired bank manager. Still, he had a very strong handshake, which I was eager to release my fingers from, and clear blue eyes that looked directly into you. As I was to understand, he was held in great respect by teachers and students alike, and perhaps this was why he could have been a retired sea captain.

One child in the class raised their hand but was not noticed until they gave a dry cough to draw the teacher's attention. When the teacher walked over to them, the girl next to the boy she had been trying to help, leaned over and whispered something in his ear, which he then wrote into his exercise book. It all seemed so obvious to me.

Children were learning or at least trying to learn and the teacher was teaching. If I could have waved a magic wand to change the modern classroom into one a hundred years earlier, nothing would have changed, except of course, for the boy with the hidden mobile phone. And so, when the bell rang to announce the lesson was over, the children waited, a little stressed they would miss time in their break, while the teacher called them to attention. All said and done, the desks were cleared as if with seconds left to live and each packed their bags and raced, although told to walk calmly, out of the room.

I walked over to the teacher and congratulated her on a job well done. It was not really, but she had followed the path laid out for her since she left university some two decades earlier, drilled in the routine to give out information, ask a few questions, give a few answers, collect the work, mark it, give it back and record the scores, keeping all about a happy average.

Such was to be her task for every lesson, like a factory worker in a processing plant: Look, Check, and Stamp. This was how education began, and how it continues with modest refinements today. Some teachers give their heart and soul to make time for the child who struggles to understand, others gave up fighting the machine that only drained their energies while they attempted to do so.

Ever the scapegoat for education's ill planning and society's too often corrupt design that causes children to be dragged through a previously unknown toxic world, the teacher's job is too little self-satisfying today.

In their defence to parents who believe it's only the teacher's responsibility to make sure their son or daughter gains top marks and ultimately a place in a better university, teachers defend their efforts by creating a defensive mechanism.

They are professionals, they would tell the world, and yet to me, they are only human beings struggling in an imperfect world, often kind, caring and loving. Most teachers I find are dedicated individuals, always seeming tired as they struggle through each lesson day by day to bring order to minds that do not want to learn, or have not been raised to know how to go beyond that of a vague response to the world before them.

It's not easy to be a teacher today, although it was not much less so in days gone by. The staffroom is not always a friendly place, with personal rivalry and bickering, no less than that found with students in a classroom or the untamed wild of the schoolyard. Seldom is there the esprit de corps that holds together a band of happy warriors, although it was so in this school.

Here teachers helped one another in the breaks, just as school friends did with the homework questions that were hastily copied and passed amongst them in the hidden corners of a corridor, on the flight of stairs when nobody was looking, or on their way home through the playing field. All hoping to have it done before they would go home and then not have to waste the time they loved best, their freedom.

Children did not love to come to school. It was just that they had no alternative. They loved or hated the children they had to share their presence within the classroom. They loved a teacher. Each would have their favourite, and each hoped that their teacher would recognise them above the rest and offer some recognition to this in the work that was returned to them. But as always, red marks were returned with each book at the beginning of each lesson. Some, admittedly, held more than others, but each was decorated with red scribbles, words that had been circled and a comment that could have been written by a doctor. "Well Done, Peter.""Could have been better, Sara.""See me after the lesson, Laura."

None did, of course, or if they did they would not really have been listening to what the teacher would say to them, as their mind would want to join their friends and not left behind as all others were moving too quickly out of the classroom. Besides, if they did miss 'their' time in the break, they would likely be late for the next lesson and this was not always a happy thought.

The best students aren't taught, I thought to myself. They teach themselves! Teachers are there for the rest. The 99% who don't want to learn or more to the point don't know how to. The trouble is that we raise children in school to believe that the teacher will do the thinking for them. We don't show them how they can be responsible for what we tell them to learn. We don't teach children how to think or how to reason better. We just expect them to do it their way and then mark and blame them for it. This is the biggest problem of school, teachers don't know what intelligence really and simply is, and so what they could so easily do to improve the work of their students.

What struck me then, and I shared this with the teacher as we walked out of the now deserted classroom together, was the difficulty of the mind of each child to know what was happening in each part of the lesson.

For sure, they would not have prepared themselves for it, and while the teacher would have remembered what the last lesson was about, few of their students would have done. One or two may have been able to say a thing, maybe two or more about the last lesson, but none could be expected to know what they had discussed three weeks earlier. Lessons, after all were something the teacher just did and their students just followed. At least, this is what they had been raised to do and so think. Few had been asked to plan their own lessons, and so create a sense of control for themselves; a control that would steer their sense of responsibility and hopefully their imagination and inspiration.

Teachers, of course, are of different personalities. Some are over accommodating, and others to be avoided by their students. None smack or cane as those of an earlier time would have done, but some can be bitterly nasty and revengeful to a student who does not fall into line quickly enough. Not all are of the 'Goodbye Mr Chips' ilk, as is hoped by students and parents alike. Some try to be, of course, and some succeed, but to do so requires a type of love that enabled them to win the long hard battles of letting young children and older students free with their own distracted energies and personality problems while keeping them close to what they were teaching them with patience and mutual respect.

All in all, teachers are just like the students they are responsible for. All are human beings trapped in a world that demands their time, energy and commitment. None are free.

Once we were in the staffroom and had found a secluded corner, I sat down while the teacher went over to make two cups of coffee. I have been trying to cut down on coffee, and at home now drink chopped up the ginger root with honey as a stimulating drink. But here, and at this time, I was glad to take the cup of coffee she offered me.

"Thank you," I said.

"So, tell me," she asked, "how do you think things went in the class?"

"Oh, I thought you tried very hard to help all the children. You made it a fun lesson. One or two of the boys got a bit restless at times."

"That's Willie and Charlie. They wind each other up a bit. But they are good kids at heart."

At heart is what teaching is all about. I thought to myself.

"Yes!" I congratulated her. "You got them under control with love and kind words rather than punishing them, which I can imagine many teachers would have done. Once you start shouting, you lose control."

She looks pleased and a little proud. She had reason to be. She handled those two very well. By her skills and not by shouting, she managed to calm them down in such a way that their minds could calmly concentrate back on the work they had been doing.

In a sort of scientific way, she had stabilised the neurotransmitters so the networks in their brain, the ways various neurons had long connected together could now recognise, associate, and process information from input to the output that they would display in the exercise book they were writing in.

"But you know," I remarked, "In that lesson, I saw something which explained to me what is wrong with every class in every country of the world. It was just a very small incident but it held the secret of how we so much fail our children."

She looked at me curiously, not sure what I was about to say.

"There was a time when you were trying to help a boy with something he did not understand. While you were doing this, another boy was stuck, and probably many more, but this boy, made a small noise to catch your attention. He made you realize that your attention needed to be split. So, naturally, you wound up your time with the first boy in order to go and help the other. This is very normal. Teaching is far more a balancing act than many realise.

But you know, what struck me was that when you left the first boy, the girl sitting next to him secretly gave him the answer. He wrote that answer in his book, without understanding why.

You see, this is what students do, really at any level! They want to present the most correct work they can so that others will not criticize them and their teacher will think better of them. It is not always just to get a better mark, although," I added this with a smile, "it too often is with younger children."

"So, when I came to mark his exercise book, all I saw was the better answer and gave him the better mark, thinking he knew what he was doing."

"It's the way of it. You did not know that he had not found that answer himself. Now, at that moment there were two boys who were struggling to understand what they were doing. But there were 37 in that class."

"35," she corrected me.

"OK, 35, but we can't assume that the remaining 33 knew exactly what they were doing, because when you come to mark their work you will not give out 35 papers marked 10/10. This causes us to realise that most of those 33 also did not know what they were doing, but for one reason or another, they struggled alone, rather than asking or waiting for your help. So, what does a student do when they are working through a question and get struck?"

"Ah! Your question is important."

"Yes. It's very important because the insight we gain from this will give us an understanding of why children get lower marks in their lessons than they could otherwise do. So, when they get stuck what can they do? What are the alternatives?" I looked at her for a response.

"Well, they can ask me for help?"

"True. But as we have seen, only two did. So, this meant that others did not want to show their classmates that they needed help, or they knew you would be too preoccupied with helping others and knew they did not have time in the lesson to wait for you. Or, they decided, they wanted to struggle alone."

"I don't know any in this class, except the girl who helped the boy, who would want to struggle alone," the teacher told me, "Most of them don't think about what they are going to do before they do it."

"Precisely," I jumped in, "This is a big thing to realise. Most do not stop and think about what they are going to do and so how they could do it before they start. So, soon after starting, they get stuck. The question then is what do they do once they get stuck?"

The teacher seemed unsure and waited for me to explain the point.

"Well, if you don't know what to do, you would check what you have got and try to see some sort of link that would bring the parts together, so that you can see how you could go forward. But we don't teach children to think like this. So," I asked her again, "what will they do?"

"Guess."

"Exactly! They will guess what to do. Now, this will not likely be a methodically worked out kind of guess. It will be more a grabbing of straws, just something that seems to fit at the moment. This is where the whole problem lies. Children are not taught how to progress through a task by themselves. They are raised to expect the teacher to do this for them, but education does not give the teacher time to do this with 35 students in a lesson.

Simply, we don't teach them how to navigate their way through information. They do not think to monitor what they are doing, and so do not make frequent checks as they move from line to line and then double-check at the solution to see if it looks kind of correct. In short, we don't teach them how to think."

"It's the way of the world." she smiled.

"It is! But if we are really to help children, then we have to help them to take control of their own learning process. Teach them to be aware of what they are doing, as they do it. Teach them to monitor their actions, and to make and keep making checks to see if things look right. Then, when they get to the end to see if they have missed something, or if they could add anything else to get that bit extra mark.

Too often, students finish a task and jump straight to the next without any consideration as to how they could have improved what they have just done. They simply wait for you to mark it and then accept what you say, but don't really consider what your advice means. If you have ever heard the statement 'we teach kids to be stupid', this is what it means. We do!"

I noticed at that moment, how more teachers seemed to be in the room than I had noticed when we first entered.

"You see," I continued, "that boy could have found out his own answer if he had kept up with what had happened in the lessons, and enjoyed the homework you gave him. Just like that girl he could have understood what happened before, so he could have understood then what to do. But he didn't, and this is why children vary in the abilities we see. In fact," – and this is a point I labour when I teach teachers– "you are not witnessing a variation of ability in your class, but a variation of confusion. The cleverest are the least confused, the majority are generally confused and the worst performers are simply the most confused as to what is going on in their lessons. If you can accept this," – I leaned slightly towards her – "then it gives you imagination and an incentive to work with this confusion rather than accepting it simply as 'their' ability. So, in truth, most in a class haven't a clue about what is really going on."

"It's true. I know it very well. I try to ask them questions to keep them on track."

"Yes, I saw that. But you see, when you asked the class of 35 (I still had the feeling it was 37 and wished I could check the register to settle my own doubt.) the mind of very many of them will be juggling with all sorts of thoughts. Oh, they will all look at you and make you think they all know the answer and want to tell you, but this is much more because they don't want others to think they don't know that answer. In fact, you found that out when you asked the question about which country had the most rain in the year."

She nodded, remembering the question.

"The first girl who had put her hand up gave the wrong answer. The second one you selected almost got it right, but you had to ask five children before you found the one who knew the correct answer. Seeing a class of hands all waving with an answer to give, does not mean they know the correct answer or that they have thought well enough before they raised their hand."

"What could I do?"

"Well, when you take over a subject or when the very first lesson of the year begins, you have to find a way of getting all in that class to be aware of what went before, so that their minds are kind of equal in understanding. Of course, the holiday disrupts things. A few might work a bit while in the break, but most will have switched off and enjoyed their life outside of school."

"We all need that!" She laughed.

I nodded and laughed a little myself.

"So, the meaning of the first few lessons after a holiday should really be about going over what happened before the holiday. It is important," I added, "that this is done in a new and interesting perspective."

"Easier said than done," she remarked, "I have to show how I am progressing too."

"Oh, I know that. But you could work it in such a way that you do progress, slowly at first, while you are going over things. You will find that once the majority, the lot," I added with a silent prayer, "are more familiar with what happened before, the faster you can proceed. I always teach through constantly refreshing sections, and indirect questions that cause them to see other associations."

"In what way?" she asked me.

"At the end of every lesson, finish with questions. Give them some sort of reward. Let the ones you select with the right answer leave the room a little earlier than the rest."

"Ah!" She smiled. "Let them escape, you mean."

I laughed too. Students little want to come to school, and the thought of finding any way to escape was always a big incentive.

"Likewise, if they can show you that they know the answers to key questions you ask then the whole class can be excused homework, after all, homework is usually useless. Students copy from each other just to give you the right answer. They will do their homework while their mind is half on other things, like watching the TV or listening to music. They seldom sit down and with real interest wonder how they can best understand the question and give you the most correct answer. Homework belongs to a time when children were required to learn by copying and remembering. We still use it today because we don't understand how to teach more efficiently."

"You mean by retracing previous lessons in the current lesson?"

I nodded. "But we also need to help them to take more of their control with the movement of information in the lesson so that they can better understand it. Get them to be more interactive, have the confidence to ask questions, but also to think about an answer before they ask that kind of thing. If we can keep their minds up to date, and constantly remind them of the rules to work with, they will, as a class, more easily produce a higher standard of work."

"But you know, some children are too far behind."

"I know, and this is where the processing image of school takes place. The survival of the fittest!"

I pulled a pen from my pocket and took a piece of paper that was lying nearby, and tried to draw how lesson content could be remembered.

"Look!" I said, "if you are in lesson five, you bring parts of lesson one and maybe lesson two into it. In the next lesson, lesson six, you bring parts of lessons three and four into that. So, lesson ten contains parts of lessons one, five and nine, and so on. This way you force their minds to re-engage old information. Oh, and never repeat it the way it was. That will be boring, and if it's boring they will have no interest to examine it in detail. If information is vaguely processed, it will be held in the short-term memory and only given a fleeting account in the long.

So, if you go over the content of an older lesson, try to present that information from a new perspective. Have parts that they recognise as belonging to something they remember. They will need this key to make better sense of it, but wrap it up with a new interest. Then they will see things they never did before."

"I know what you mean. It's like when you do something again then things can click into place."

"So, imagine the mind of that boy. He was stuck and did not know how to proceed. He asked you for help. You came and explained the problem the way you had understood it. But for that boy at that moment, he could not lock into your thoughts. There can be a thousand reasons for this. He may have liked you so much that he was thinking about you and not what you were saying. Equally, he could have disliked you or felt uncomfortable with you, but I doubt that." I smiled. (She was a very kind lady.) "Perhaps, he was thinking about someone else in the class or maybe something outside of school. The mind is always 'living' with information, and because he could not recognise what to do at that very moment with this problem, his mind drifted to something else. It did not naturally drift back, just because you came to help him. Learning is not so simple."

"So, what happened?"

"Well, he had been in the class long enough to understand some parts of the problem. It was just that he missed a link or maybe two to see how all things ran together. I bet that if you had had enough time alone with him, you could have nudged his mind to discover that link, and maybe more so that suddenly everything would make sense. The problem is that with so many other children, you seldom have that time."

"So, what's the solution?"

"Like I said, firstly repeat parts of earlier lessons as you progress with each one. Then, well then, you will have to try to do what his parents had not."

"What is that?"

"Teach him how to think!"

"You make it sound so easy."

"In a way it is. It's not rocket science to teach a child how to think. You simply need to cause him or her to be really aware of what is happening at any moment. Train them to be sensitive. You know, most people on this planet walk around with half of their brain switched off, well; civilisation has cultivated them to be this way.

You know, routine jobs, mindless television, simple entertainment, that sort of thing, but let's not go into that now."

"You make it sound as if the school does it too."

"Have no doubt about it, it does!"

"How do you mean, we don't teach children how to learn?"

"Well you might, but most teachers I know do not. They simply give out information, check if everyone seems to understand it, devise some sort of test and evaluate the ability of each to have understood that information. This is not teaching children how to learn. It's only processing them on the ability they have developed so far, or their desire to really want to know this information, or, and this is really important, the distractions they can overcome to concentrate as information unfolds. This is not teaching children to learn. Oh! We call it so, but it is not.

Now think of every single child in that class you had. Think of their minds all buzzing with different thoughts every second. One will be focusing on the book they are reading then suddenly their thoughts will shoot off to wonder what the boy over there is thinking if the girl over there likes him, how long it will be before the lesson finishes and if he can get something from the school shop.

The mind is never still, and it's not easy for it to stay focused unless it is continually entertained. This is one reason why the teacher who is loved, happy, joking, and tells interesting stories is a real teacher because they know how to capture the hearts of their learners. Do you think the girl who told that boy the answer, after you left him, is cleverer than he is?"

"Well! She always gets better marks. She's quite clever."

"Clever has nothing to do with it. Children are not clever or stupid. They are all just developing through life as it comes to them. Some will recognise things easier because they are happier, more interested. With this interest, comes a skill in recognising how parts of information match and the outcomes that can be predicted from them. The more practice they have with this, the better they become. Thinking, what you might call intelligence, is only a huge number of skills the individual has built up.

It just means that this girl had a richer mind development than this boy. Now, I don't know when it started. It may have started soon after she was born. There again, something last year may have suddenly 'switched on' a deep desire to be involved with the world about her. Perhaps, she saw a movie and found a purpose for her life in one of the characters. A purpose she realized she could manifest by being good in her subjects at school. Who knows what switches children on, or any student for that matter, but we need to find ways to help them all to want to learn."

A friend of mine once told me about her son. Hisham was about ten at the time. He had found a way to make money by selling things to a shop. The shop owner was very impressed with this child and said to him, "If you come to work for me, we can make a lot of money together."

Hisham replied, "Do you think I am crazy. Why should I give up my school? It's the only way for me to succeed in life!"

"I bet his mother was behind that!" said the teacher.

I nodded, half in acknowledgement to myself. I knew she was.

"You know," she told me, "in every parent evening, some parents turn up just because they have to. Show face, you know! But I can see they are not really interested in doing anything themselves to help their child. They just believe it's all up to me. And when their child does not get top marks, they come and blame me."

I understood her feelings.

"Well, parents are cultivated by society to think you will do everything that is needed for their child's education. They see themselves as responsible just for the health and happiness of their child. The learning part is up to the school. Not all think like this, of course, and it's the better educated who know the reality of school life and the part they have to play."

"Of course, I do get parents who do ask me what they can do."

"I know. The problem is really ignorance. Not all parents understand what learning means. We really need a full-scale educational program to help parents understand how they can be more responsible for their child's educational development."

"Cartoons would be a good idea."

"You took the thought right out of my mind," I said adding "and broadcast just before nightly soap operas to catch their attention.

"That would be something, wouldn't it?"

A teacher had been watching us for some time, and as I invited her to join us, four or five also sat down near us.

"Excuse me," said one, "I could not help but overhear that you were talking about children's intelligence. Have you heard of Howard Gardner?"

"Yes. I have," I replied. "But why do you ask me this?" (Although, I knew what was coming.)

"Gardner's famous you know! After all, he realized there are nine bits of intelligences and not just one."

"So, I understand," I replied. "But may I ask you, how does this make any difference to the way you have taught today?"

It was to be a general question, and so my view moved slowly and questioningly to every teacher around us.

None of the assembled teachers could tell me. Yet, all too often teachers use Gardner's nine bits of intelligences as a battle cry seeking to impress others that they are up to date, and so know what they are doing.

This was the angle I was looking for. Here was a way I could help them to understand what was wrong with the ways they had been trained in their beginnings, or influenced by the various courses they had been sent on or even joined at their own expense, as they struggled to discover new ways to help their students perform better.

"Tell me," I asked of them, "What use are the nine bits of intelligences to you as a teacher. They may be of great interest to a psychologist, but how do they help you in your task to develop information with 30 or 40 students in 45 minutes?"

I did not wait for a response; for I could see that none would be forthcoming.

However, at that very moment, the door to the staffroom burst open, as a teacher in her early thirties came in. Red-faced and all too clearly frustrated, she threw herself down into a chair and muttered to no one and to all, "Little Bastards!"

The other teachers did not stir. They had been there before and knew she just needed time to cool off. After a few moments, a colleague placed a cup of coffee on the table in front of her, to which she replied with a tired look of gratitude.

We left her to get it out of her system. No one blamed her, and so I continued.

"You know, all Gardner did was to suggest we have nine different ways of developing our intelligence. So, he suggests we have linguistic intelligence, the kind used by a lawyer or writer.

Mathematical intelligence displayed by logical thinking people. Spatial intelligence like a chess player has.

Not only are these all developmental, in that they are not inherited features that derive from nine different genes, but not one of these bits of intelligences explains to you why the student of mathematics does not understand how to correctly solve an algebraic problem. Or, why the student of English spells words wrongly or presents their mind less competently than another. Or, why one student in Geography explained that Jurassic was a period of the Palaeozoic era when it was actually of the Mesozoic and this because Jurassic was the only period they could think of because they remembered the movie, Jurassic Park.

Most importantly, none of Gardner's bits of intelligences assists the teacher to know why or how to improve the performance of students who just failed their physics test. Yet, teachers, I met constantly ask me if I know of Gardner's nine intelligences as if knowledge of these offers the solution to better education. They do not."

"What could do," I continued because each was now listening very keenly to what I was saying, "is a new way of looking at intelligence that does give the teacher a hands-on approach to changing the ability of their students. It would be a method that sees the brain developing through the environment, as its mind struggles to design its efficiency. This would not see human intelligence and the environment as two separate features, but as intelligence coming into existence and living through the environment.

In this way, each individual sees their own perspective of the world, which they learn to share with others through language. It's for this reason that I see intelligence as a language process based on and controlled by the emotional sensitivity of the individual. Fix the heart, and you fix the brain!" I added, as I explained this to them.

"What has the heart got to do with the ability of the child to think?" interrupted a teacher, in her early 40s.

"Think of the brain simply as a processing system," I asked of her.

"The mind directs the brain's sensors to analyze information. The brain will store what the mind has found most interesting to it. When the mind is aware of further information or a problem to solve, it will access the brain's memory banks for the most relevant information. Now! The mind is driven by the chemistry of the body. You can see this with the effect of a drug. Too simply," I added, "the behaviour of others cause us to be happy or feel unhappy. When we are happy, chemicals work smoothly in our brain to allow it to work as efficiently as it has developed to do so. But affect the harmony of those chemicals, with stress, abuse, bullying, boredom or even unhappiness, and they play havoc with the mind's ability to learn!"

A beam of acceptance came from her eyes. She already knew this and was sounding me out. I knew it. She knew that I knew it. We bonded in a common cause. But I continued to address the others in the staffroom with the opening she had given me.

"Once you realise this view of intelligence, then all you have to do is teach in a way that stimulates the student's happy emotions, make them feel secure, give them a purpose to learn what you intend to share with them, and most importantly work with the language skills they have developed. If this were more realized today, many of the problems we have with students would not be so impossible to deal with, as we have been impressed to believe. Children, students, they are just human beings, and human beings just need love. Base your teachings more on love than assessment and you will be amazed as to what you achieve."

"Have you had the experience of this?"

"About 40 years," I responded, with a quite almost embarrassed smile.

The room seemed to laugh, as teachers from other parts of it drifted towards us. I had left my books on a table, and one teacher now held one of these on her knee, as she asked me, "Do you think we are responsible for the ability of our students?"

"Not entirely," I said gently, "It's a shared responsibility with the parents to better guide the developing knowledge and awareness of the student, and of course, to give them the purpose to want to develop."But then I told them the story of Jamie Escalante. A modern-day teacher who refused to let his 16-year-old Hispanic street kids be the failure society expected of them, and drilled them in their school work and pulled parents into help, so that all passed their finals with high grades. I watched each of the faces around me as the story helped them to see, just what the teacher really could achieve if they have a mind to.

"So, what happens if a student is dyslexic?" The question came from someone in the background.

"The problem is to really know why they appears to be dyslexic. You know, to have the gene for dyslexia, which is a very rare occurrence, does not mean that it will be active within the child's DNA. I have met so many children diagnosed by the school psychologist or a well-intentioned teacher, who suspected a child, had such a gene because they seemed unable to spell correctly or had trouble with words. Yet, with all the children I have met, their problem was not inborn but environmental. It was just a question of correcting their very long development and this was usually rooted in some emotional pain."

"You know," interrupted a teacher, "I've had it with that class." It was the woman who had entered the room shortly before and had now joined us.

"What happened?" I asked.

"Oh! I can't stand it anymore. One little so and so threw her shoe at me."

I looked at the woman; a nice, kind, caring human being driven to her limit by small children who had no sense of control.

"I've an idea," I prompted, "Take control of their energies, instead of giving into them."

"What do you mean?" she said.

"OK, try this. When you next enter the classroom, go in like a whirlwind. Don't give them a chance to think or to play up. The little girl who threw her shoe at you was probably just playing for attention; first to get you angry, and then to use this to amuse the other children. So, the very instant you enter the classroom be very excited and happy."

She looked at me wondering which planet I had come from.

"Get them to move fast, but safely. Play a game to get them moving about and so use their energies. If it's safe, running to different walls, touch North, touch West, that kind of thing. If not, get them to jump up and down to see who can jump the highest. Once, they have burned off some of that crazy energy, get them to play statues. The one who moves first is the loser. This will get them to calm down. Then give them tasks, so each feels they are doing something to help you. Then, you have control over them, and then they will listen to what you want to teach them."

"Might work," she thought aloud. "Thanks, I'll try it."

We talked for a little bit longer and in leaving, I promised I would come again. The drive home seemed a long one. My mind was on many things, not least the numerous ones I had to do tomorrow.

Chapter Three
The Mother

Indeed, it had been a busy day. The morning had gone so fast, I hardly had time to reply to the many emails in my Inbox. In fact, it was just as I began to attempt to do this that the telephone rang. Immediately, I recognized the voice of the teacher I had spoken to the day before, only now she sounded confident and even a little excited.

"Well, I've got to tell you what happened!" she began, "When I entered that classroom, everything was in a mess. You can't imagine what it was like; kids screaming and running about. One was standing at the teacher's table, Food, water, papers all over the desks and floor. You can't imagine the Hell; chaos is just not the word!" She gave a small, half-repressed wicked kind of sound.

"So, as you said, I quickly took charge. I didn't give the real troublemakers a chance to think." Quickly, I pointed to each one of them and said, "Look! You are my teachers today. I want you to help me."

They said, "Yes, What can we do?"

I said, "You! (To the worst troublemaker) You are in charge of this group of kids." I pointed to one area of children. To another troublemaker, I said, "You are in charge of this area," and so on with the other three worst kids.

"Now," I said to them, "before we can do all these great activities I have here in my hand (I had made some A3 sheets with things for them to learn), we have to clean this whole room. Pick up the papers, clear the food, and then we will arrange the desks in the way your group likes them to be. Do this as quickly as you can. Then come back to me, so you can help me with these games I have made."

Well! Something magic happened. It was a miracle, I know it. I was so stressed at night because I had to meet this class again.

Immediately, the kids who were always fighting me and throwing things around became super six-year-old managers. They got their friends to tidy up, clear the mess and have all sitting expectantly behind their desks. They had found a new game to play; only they didn't know it was my game. Anyway, this took about ten minutes, then the leaders came to me and I gave them each an activity sheet. "This is for you," I said, and to another, "This for you," and so on. "You have to distribute this activity sheet to everyone in your group and they must use their books because what you see on the activity sheet is from their books.

Now, everyone in your group has to ask you a question. But I don't want them all to ask the same question. Everyone has to think of a different question about something on the activity sheet. I will be watching, and if you or someone else in the group doesn't know the answer, raise your hand and I will come and tell it to you. Everyone has to be responsible to everyone in their group. Make sure everyone understands the activity sheet and reviews it."

So, for example, the first worksheet asks, "Tell me countries and their capitals?"

So, the children have to ask you, "Is Paris the capital of France?" You and the other children have to answer, "Yes! The capital of France is Paris."

If they ask you, "Is the capital of Germany, China?" Then you say, "No! China is a country. The capital of Germany is Berlin," The kids laughed and ran to their group.

Now! Shirley, the naughtiest one, well she managed this best! After she had asked all her students a question, she ticked their names and then she gave them a star. She was doing it exactly the way I would do it. She was being just like me. I loved her. And, if a student did not answer correctly, then she came to me and reported them. "Look," she told me, "he (she) didn't know. Remind me? What shall I tell him?" It was incredible! All the children were helping each other. The whole class was productive. They were working together.

The most aggressive one, Jasmine, began by pushing the kids in her group, but then I said to her, "No! Not like that. Let us tell them first, and then let them repeat it." She changed from being a bully to being a helper. It was amazing! For the first time, I left that classroom with a happy smile on my face. It was great! Now, I can use this responsibility to tame them so that there is only one leader. And that, she told me with a lot of confidence, will be me.

I was really happy to hear this. We spoke for a few moments and then I had to excuse myself, for the door opened and in walked a lady in her mid-thirties.

I had actually been looking forward to meeting this lady all day, because her request had a sense of urgency about it. I stood up and moved to greet her and, after the usual exchange of names, welcomed her to sit down. She took a chair facing my desk, but before I had a chance to sit down myself she suddenly blurted out her concern.

"Excuse me. But I have to know what my son's IQ is. I'm worried he is not clever enough."

"Can you please tell me?" Her eyes showed signs of tiredness and stress.

"Why do you want to know this?" I asked, slightly taken aback by the abruptness of her manner.

The woman looked tense, and with lines of stress, began to explain to me how her son was failing in school. She was worried about why he was not getting good marks and if he would be able to get into university.

I looked into the mother's eyes. She looked so desperate, frightened even. She just wanted a number to believe in. Something she could know, that would make everything all right for her son.

I adjusted my position in the chair to which I had now returned and asked if she would like a cup of tea. She nodded a little nervously and waited while I asked my secretary to bring in a fresh pot with two cups. I rested my hands upon the top of the desk before me, and asked her to tell me about her son.

"He's 15," she told me, "He's a good boy. He does not get into trouble, and comes home early every night."

"What does he like best in school?" I asked.

"Well, he doesn't seem to like anything special," and then added, as if to reassure me he is a good student, "But he tries you know. He really does."

There was a slight knock on the door before it gently opened. Alice came in with a tray and placed it on my desk in a way that did not disturb the various papers lying about.

"And, what's his name?" I asked.

"Peter. He's my eldest son. Can you tell me his IQ?" she repeated the question with urgency.

So many parents have asked me the same thing. I picked up the teapot and poured it into her cup. In giving the cup and saucer to the mother, I asked,

"Do you think it's important to know your son's IQ?"

She looked at me a little puzzled.

"Then, I would know if he will be OK in his big exams."

Her face took on a kind of strange look as if I had not realized this.

"A number will not tell you how your son will perform in a test," I told her.

"But it would mean he would be clever enough to get into university," She responded.

"Well, there is a great myth about IQ, you know; for a start and to be very honest. You cannot measure intelligence."

The mother now looked at me with suspicion, as if she had come to see the wrong person.

"Look," I said quietly. "We have brain cells and we have chemicals between them. Change the chemicals, and the signal moving through the brain cells will be affected. This is exactly what happens when our emotions change. When we are happy and interested, these chemicals, we call them neurotransmitters; conduct the signals through the networks of the brain according to the ways they have developed to structure themselves."

"What do you mean developed?" The suspicion in her face had changed to one of puzzlement as her eyebrows frowned, but the tone of her question still belayed a lingering suspicion.

"Well," I began to explain a little deeply how we actually think, "The networks related to how we understand the information we receive from our senses, like when we see things or hear sounds, are built up through experiences. The basic formation of these networks begins while the baby is still in the womb."

The mother suddenly changed her face to one of interest now.

"What do you mean inside the womb?"

"Well, the intelligence of the child doesn't begin weeks after birth when they can respond to simple games their parents play with them. Long before this and while in the womb, the brain of the unborn baby will begin to build up a basic way to handle sounds through those it hears about the mother, and sight from the defused light that enters the embryonic sac. According to the emotional chemicals, it receives from the mother, by the happiness or stress in her life, the foetus will start to devise a way of regulating its brain chemistry to relate to and classify information. All these acts create the foundation blocks that the baby will build upon after birth, as they begin to make sense of the world about them."

"You mean, if I was stressed when I was carrying my son, he would have known this?"

"Of course, your son was a part of you in all ways at that time. But don't worry about this, as a normal human being your emotions will move up and down, and at this stage of its development, the foetus is only setting up a temporary system of processing information. It is their experiences after birth that will far more importantly set the levels by which their neurotransmitters are produced, and so how sensitive they will become as they understand things."

This was getting a bit too much for the mother. She had never heard thoughts like this, and she needed a break to make sense of what I had told her, so I asked, "Tell me, does Peter have any brothers or sisters?" (I had gathered that he had a least one younger brother.)

"He has an older sister and a younger brother, Jill and Martin."

"How does he get on with them?"

"Jill's like a mother to him. She always has been. But Martin, well you know boys, always fighting."

I nodded my head in sympathy to help her feel more relaxed.

"It's good you have Jill, I think." I remarked with a smile that prompted the mother to relax. She gave a slight laugh in return.

"But it's really easy to understand all this," I continued. "You see, brain cells receive information according to how well they have developed to recognise it, and remember the role of the chemicals in this…" – I gave her a slight nod –"…they will devise areas of relative information."

"What! You mean like categorising."

I saw the sparkle in her eyes. She was beginning to understand.

"Exactly, so, if you go back to the very first stage after birth, your son would have been developing a skill at telling the differences between basic outlines. Just simple lines and things like the corners of a wall for instance. The horizontal and vertical lines of a window, even the outline shape of curtains in the room. The newborn has to learn to understand what information is, and this is how they start.

You can see this in the eyes of newborns. Their eyes are not as fluid in movement as they become a little later, as ours are. A newborn's eyes lock from one object to another, as their brain takes in information to learn to define basic shapes. Upon this, they begin to understand the world about them, and then when they go to school, the letters of the alphabet and how these combine to make different words. Dyslexia is really a problem with keeping order with letters."

Something changed in the manner of the mother when I said the word dyslexia. There was a momentary tenseness in her body but she hid it quickly, and I felt this was somewhere I should not go, at least not now. So, I continued as if this had not been noticed.

"How well your child understood the way things were explained to him in the past (and this goes right back to birth), will depend upon the ways he has developed to recognise and process information today. At least, that is until his mind is affected by stress, anxiety or fear, because then chemicals in his brain associated with these feelings will interfere with the signals that move through the brain cells, and this will cause him difficulty to pay attention, keep his interest and to understand the meaning of a lesson. It's the same for all of us. This is what makes us human, which is why both parents and teachers need to realise the importance of happiness in the development of intelligence because positive thoughts release chemicals that help in the learning process."

"Yes! But that wouldn't affect the way he was born would it?" It was half a statement and half a question.

I distracted the intensity of her obvious concern by pouring tea into my cup.

"Well actually, there's no way to know the intelligence of a child when they are born. We cannot measure the genetic value of intelligence."

"I thought you could!"

"So do many people, but it's a myth. Look!" I told her, "we inherit genetic codes, but these codes only give our brain the instructions for how to form in a very basic sense. The genes interact with proteins to make anything happen and proteins are affected by a cup of coffee." My thoughts drifted to what I wished I was drinking, instead of this tea.

"There's no way we can stop the workings of a child's mind, open up their brain and find the genes inside. We simply cannot know what the intelligence of an individual is genetically. Although, for very political reasons many psychologists have said they can. But the truth is they cannot.

Anyway, as far as neurons are concerned, brain cells that are, they develop through two kinds of networks, radial and tangential. Radial follows a genetic framework; while tangential develop through signals from the environment. Most of the networks relating to how the brain processes information form through signals from the environment, what we see and what we hear. So, while it's important that children get the right nutrition, their brain can better form, it's also and I believe more important to train their senses to be more aware in their understanding of things."

"Isn't it more important to give them the right kind of food? I always gave my children a good breakfast when they were young. Mind you," she hesitated for a moment, "now we have to get off to work so early in the morning, the kids look after themselves."

"Do they eat breakfast? They should do, you know. It's very important for them. Their brain needs fuel to burn if it's to work."

She looked a bit sheepish at this.

"Well, most times, they get something in school. You see, it's a struggle to get them into bed and so they are tired when they wake up, and I have to go to work early."

"So, what time do they eat?"

"The break is at eleven o'clock."

I did not reply, but many things were beginning to fall into place. Nutrition is important, but less than the drive of the individual and this comes from the guidance, time given and love of the parents.

"I have done a lot of research, spent over 30 years, understanding how the mind drives the brain. We say psychology over physiology. In other words, if the child is correctly motivated and given a clear language to understand the meaning of information, they will give that energy to force their brain cells into the better networks that enable them to understand better. You could say be more clever."

"Mr Andersen," she used my name for the first time.
"Please, Roy is OK," I insisted.

"Roy, I don't understand why you keep talking about language. I mean we all talk English in our family and school. Mind you, Jill is learning French."

"Well, Jean, May I call you Jean, please?"

The mother nodded, and I suddenly realized that her entrance into the room had been so swift that too little time had been given to understanding each other.

"Jean, language is really about how we share our mind with another. It's not just the names we give to things or what those things do. It's more about how we place our emotions into them, the gestures we use and the way we tell the story behind them. Sensitivity in expression and so storytelling has a lot to do with this. Have you heard of the 30 million word gap?" I asked her.

I could see from the way Jean was looking that she was asking herself if she knew 30 million words.

"No," I interrupted her thoughts to explain what I meant. "A long study on young children was made in 1994, which proved that according to the intellectual background and effort of the parents, children as young as four could know some 30 million words more than other children of the same age, depending upon the language skills they had been raised on by their parents."

"30 Million seems incredible," She looked at me.

"I don't know how they defined a word and probably included phonemes, but the real meaning here is not that such children had a greater vocabulary, but that they would have been raised with a certain discipline to concentrate and be more able to expand upon their feelings as they could associate faster to what the teacher in school would be talking about. So, these children would begin school better prepared for it, and would most likely be the better students right throughout their school career."

"Just because their parents taught them more words?" Jean looked a little suspiciously at me.

I nodded. "Performance in school really comes down to how the parents prepare their child for school and mentally support them through it."

I looked at her for a moment, struggling to know how to explain what I knew easily and readily for her.

"Look!" I said, "We've been told a great lie. We are told that we have police to protect us, doctors for our health and teachers to educate our children. But the reality is that one teacher does not have time to educate 30 or 40 children at the same time. The ability of those children to pay attention and interact with the information the teacher is giving to them largely depends on the ways they have been taught to think, and the sense of self-discipline to concentrate on what is happening they have acquired from their parents.

This is often reflected in the academic background of the parents because those who have been through university know the teacher in school does not have the time to really educate their child and so the responsibility they have in this. Lesser educated parents mistakenly assume the teacher is paid to make all the education for their child. Mind you," I added, "the kind of job the parents do also plays a part in this."

"How do you mean?" She looked at me curiously.

"Well, the job we do causes us to develop our thinking in specific ways. You might say, for instance, that in order to keep our job, we develop sensitivity with the world of that job, after all, if we do not make an effort we would lose out to someone else in the promotion game or worse still lose the job for not being efficient enough. So, we learn to think in different ways according to the job we do. A doctor will think in a different way to a policeman, just as a policeman will to a carpenter."

"My husband's a carpenter."

"So was I once, a long time ago. But we are talking here only about how sensitive the job requires your thinking to be, and so how it can condition you in this. So, the job teaches people different ways of understanding information and also a new level of sensitivity. In one sense, this cultivated mind is the mind that raises the children once they come home from work."

"Do you mean that a child learns their intelligence from the job the parents do?"

"In one sense, yes, but in the larger picture the child learns to understand their world through the friends and interests they have, and the people they meet with the things they do. This is very complex to understand and another reason why intelligence can't be measured. The environment of each individual is so different from any other that we cannot classify the environment for intelligence. It's not specific things, but a multitude of things that interact in a gigantic puzzle; with the emotional drive of each setting their own level of interaction as the individual is inspired by one factor and deterred by another.

"You mean intelligence doesn't have anything to do with school grades?" queried Jean.

I shook my head, "Not for the normally born child. No. Our whole understanding of genetic diversity is wrong when it comes to intelligence. As I have just explained, school works on language and emotion and neither of these are affected by genetic diversity. Every single human being inherits the same genetic value for these features, which…" – I paused for a moment – "…are the base upon which they can build their intelligence."

"But I heard something about a book called the 'Bell Curve' that said that IQ is inherited."

"The first thing to understand is that IQ is not intelligence. IQ is just an abbreviation for the Intelligence Quotient, which is a theory of how to calculate intelligence. IQ is only a method. It is not the function of intelligence, and it does not give any indication of how intelligence comes to be or where it comes from. Yet, without understanding this, so many people including very famous psychologists, mistakenly and unknowingly say IQ when they mean intelligence. They are not the same."

"I didn't know."

I half raised my eyebrows as I dropped my head and smiled a little as if to indicate that she was not alone.

"Forget 'The Bell Curve'," I suggested. "It was written as a political argument to limit the opportunities of African Americans and Hispanics in the American society. Too little of the data used matched up, and too many comments were wrongly asserted. The authors were simply playing with politics."

"No! This was not about politics. It was about how IQ was different in different people."

I considered the innocence in the woman and wondered how much I could explain to her in the short time we had.

"Step outside of the picture." I drew my hand from where it was laying on the desk and pulled it up into the air to emphasise coming out of something.

"The whole history of education is based on creating differences within children, to control the roles they will later play in their society."

"Yes, I know about that," she told me, "But that was a long time ago. Now, we have equal opportunity for all children."

I looked at the clock on the wall. Our time was quickly running short and I did not have the time to explain what she did not understand. I wanted to know more about Peter, but I struggled to correct her thinking.

"I have written 13 books explaining how education works. It may seem that there is equality in education today, but there are many strategies laid deeply within it that ensure it is not. Basically, let's say language comes down to how the child's mind has learned to be sensitive to understand things, and how they explain their mind to another. You know, there are so many kids in every class who know the right answer. But because most of them don't know the right way to explain their thoughts, they are judged as only partially understanding and so given a lower score than they would otherwise get if they had known better how to explain their mind. It all comes down to language.

It is for this very reason that I always advise teachers never to accept a child's response of 'I don't know' to a question they ask them, and to teach them to respond with 'I don't understand the question'. The 'I don't know' response seals the interaction causing the teacher to move the question to the next student, but the 'I don't understand the question' causes, let's say forces the teacher to present their mind in another way that both develops the language ability of the student and the teacher, but enables the student to present a reasonable answer and gain confidence by doing so. They learn! Otherwise, they do not.

We may understand from this that school is not about intelligence, and so why we are wrong to think that some children are brighter, faster and smarter than others on account of some inborn quality.

These top students simply kept up with information as it continually advanced. For whatever reason, filled by the tempered drive of a parent or their own desire to 'win', they worked hard to understand and practice the content of each lesson and kept up as one lesson went to the next. This is why they know the answer faster and more accurately than the rest in the class. In truth, their brain became more proficient, but not because it was born this way. It simply developed to be so, as they pushed their networks to expand and associate better with a variety of information in different contexts."

Jean was obviously struggling to understand how a child could be better than another, just because they had found some secret about learning that others had not.

"Look," I told her, "Einstein once said of the school, 'You have to learn the rules of the game, and then you have to learn to play them better than anyone else'."

The puzzled expression remained on her face, so I had to explain to her what most people really do not know or understand.

How School Works:

"Being good in school is to be good in the two languages school works upon. These are mathematics and the language used by the country to educate its children. This would be English for British children, German for German children, Arabic for Middle Eastern children, although, it may be English for Kashmiri children.

The important thing to realise is that language works on rules. The problem is that there are very many of these rules and if the child does not keep up with them, as most do not because their mind drifts or they are worried about something in their life as most children do, then they become confused about how to think with what to do when they are working through a problem or trying to describe some event.

A child who missed some rule that explained how to move numbers about in maths, or a child who missed some rule that explains how to use an adjective correctly will be confused to know what to do when they need to do this.

So, will they put their hand up and wait for the teacher to come and explain to them what they do not understand? Some will, of course, but then how well will they relate to what the teacher is saying when the teacher tries to hurriedly explain what needs more time but this time they don't have because they are trying to rush about to help many children who also do not understand. Or will the child look at what the child next to them is doing and copy from them so they appear to keep up?

Remember, students tend to fear to appear to be less than others because of the competitive attitude of a class. Or will they simply and just 'blindly guess' what to do, sometimes being correct but more often not. Either way not knowing or learning what they are doing for the next occasion when they will come across a similar situation.

So, for all those who do not understand what to do, or can gain a clear understanding from the teacher or other students at the moment in time, they fumble through their lessons obtaining marks of 7 or 8 out of 10 that show they are not very good or marks of 4 or 5 to show the teachers are not very bad!

After all, if teachers marked many students with 1 or 2 out of 10, they would soon be out of a job, just as their school would soon earn a poor reputation. So, teachers mark a very few of their students as excellent and most about the average, but never zero even when the child understands almost nothing in their lesson."

"But these rules don't explain how much the child knows, do they?" Jean looked at me less puzzlingly but still unsure she understood what I had told her.

"Well, they do as far as maths is concerned," I told her. "Because the child who does not know how to move information in the clear way demanded by maths, will get the wrong answer. Look, let me show you." I picked up a pen and wrote the following equation on a piece of paper lying next to me.

6/2 (2+1) =

"What is the answer? Well, this equation appeared on Facebook and actually, a lot of teachers got it wrong.

You see, they said to themselves, let's do the brackets first. So, 2 + 1 = 3. Then, let's multiply 3 by 2 so we get 6, and then divide 6 by 6 to get 6/6 = 1. But 1 is the wrong answer.

You see, this rule of maths called BODMAS, is always to begin with the brackets but to work through the equation from the left. Those who knew this rule firstly did the brackets to get 3. Then they worked from the left, and so divided 6 by 2 to get 3. Then, they multiplied 3 by 3 to give the answer of 9, which is correct.

The very important thing to understand here is that all those who gave the answer of 1, were not stupid. They were not of low intelligence. They very simply did not know or had forgotten 'the rule'! So, a student who knows the rules of maths will be very good at maths. They will also," I added, "be very good in physics and chemistry because these use formulas and equations that rely upon the rules of maths."

A spark came to Jean's eyes. "Well, this does not explain why they will be good in History," she told me feeling she could defend her own ability to think.

"In one way, you are right," I told her, "But you see, a child who has learned the rules to spell a word and has learned all the grammar to make a good sentence construction will be able to present a very correct mind, especially if they are good at storytelling, and this will encourage the teacher to give them a good mark. They can explain very clearly the events behind some battle or the nitrogen cycle in biology," I added.

When the student gets a good mark and they like the teacher, they will be encouraged to try to learn the subject matter, because they believe they have a chance. You must remember that the classroom is a very competitive environment. The best student is doing all they can to stay the best, and others will try to be like them or believe that they never can be.

"I never thought much of myself in school," Jean interrupted me.

"Nor did I as a child," I told her, "but this confidence to believe in your ability is the very most important thing to the student in their learning, because it gives them the confidence to try to sort things out for themselves to want to succeed. I was so very bad at maths in school. I really was always lost and getting very low marks, until I had a new teacher. This teacher was calm, always inspiring. He would come up to me and help me to understand what the question was really asking of me, but do you know the most important thing he ever did?" I looked at her.

Jean shook her head.

"He said to me 'you can do this'. It was never said in a strong instructional way. Just a kind passive way that seemed to settle into my mind. He did this occasionally, but I noticed how I began to think that if this great maths teacher said to me that I can do this, then, he knows, so I can. From that moment onwards happy confidence began to grow in me with the realisation that I could do whatever the question was asking of me. Once I began to think like this, I began to see the question not as a complexity of information that made no sense, but as a game. A game, I could win. All I needed to do was to discover where the hidden parts were to play the game.

Well, the whole story is that at 17 years of age I left school having failed arithmetic. They said I was not clever enough to take the final maths exam. But I went back to school when I was 20, without really knowing what a fraction was. Because of this great maths teacher," I emphasised the word teacher– "I discovered that I could think and I could think very well in maths. In fact, I eventually obtained a 92% pass in Applied Mathematics just below university level, because of this teacher, nothing else."

"You mean," she asked, "your whole ability changed in maths just because this one teacher gave you the belief that you could do maths?"

I smiled at Jean and nodded my head. "It's really as simple as this. He was a great teacher. Not because he knew how to make the subject he was teaching easy to understand, but because he gave me the belief that I could do the problems I was confronted with. And," I added, "because I believed him I did, and I became very, very good at maths. But you see this brings us to the other part of the story of the school, because while the school works on languages and these work on rules, all of these rely upon the emotional stability and drives of the individual student."

"Do you mean if they are happy?" She asked.

"Well, this is a big misunderstanding in education. You see, the school used to be based on instruction, memorising and punishment. If you did not remember what you were told to remember you were punished," – I paused for a moment – "In fact, I find there are still teachers who use this methodology today.

I found it in India and Kashmir. Students were physically hit if they could not remember things. Their teachers believed they were being lazy and punished them for being so. But this is so counterproductive once you begin to understand how the chemistry of the brain reacts to ill-treatment. It literally stops thinking! Anyway," I continued. "A movement began in school in the 1970s that believed the child could learn better if they were happy and learned by themselves. This became very misunderstood by many teachers who thought the only thing that is important is for the child to be happy and creative.

In one sense, they did become happier and more creative, but they did not learn any better because to make them happier teachers stopped teaching them the rules of the languages I have just explained. So, they did not know how to think within the world of school. Smart kids remained distinct from the average, and the average varied from those who understood most to those who do not seem to understand anything."

"So, what do you mean by emotion?"

"Everything begins in the home. It is so important the child feels emotional security in the home, parents who are not too critical of them and certainly not fighting and causing disruption to the peace and calm of the home environment. Equally, the child needs to feel secure outside of their home and so they should be guided with the kind of children they mix with and share their free time with. Inside the classroom, which is again a very competitive place, they need to feel respect from others for who they are.

They need to believe in their ability and to have supportive friends. They need to feel they can talk and even politely disagree with what the teachers say, but most importantly they need their purpose. What do they want to do after school? Do they want to be a doctor? A computer engineer? or even an astronaut? This purpose, often seeded by the parents, is the most important driving factor for the student. Otherwise, they are in their lessons, listening, reading, and doing assignments and their homework because they have to! There is no inner drive to be better, to give more care and attention to the work they hand in.

So, all in all, the performance of the student in school lies in how well the parents have prepared them before school, how they assist them throughout their school career, how the student is able to avoid or counter the many distractions and fears that will play on their mind, the quality of the teachers they will encounter and the inspirations they will receive along the way that fuels their purpose to win the game."

Chapter Four
The Son

The clock on the wall was drawing my attention again, as I could feel the minutes racing too quickly, and felt the urgency to bring our time to focus on Jean's concern.

"I would like to hear more about Peter."

"Well, this is about Peter, isn't it?" she asked me, "I mean his schooling."

"In a broad sense, but if I am to help you I need to know more about your son."

"He can't spell!" she blurted out. It was an open confession, and her face fell when she said it.

"Have you been told Peter's dyslexic?"

She nodded in silence. But it was the single tear she tried to hold back, that ran slowly down her right cheek that told its own story.

"You see," she muttered, "it's my fault."

Now, it was my turn to look puzzled.

"Why do you think this is your fault?"

"The psychologist said it was inherited. It means I passed it on to my son."

"Oh no! This is absolutely not true." There was a surge of anger that rose up inside me to protect this mother and deal with the ignorance behind her stress.

"Look! I want to get to the bottom of this. Can you bring Peter in to meet me?"

Things came and went and it was almost a week before Jean returned with her son but I'd been thinking deeply about this mother and the devastation she felt. I was eager to meet her son if only to resolve the stress that had built up within her.

On Tuesday morning, Jean was my first appointment, and I had come to the office early to clear up the various things that usually hindered the start of a good day.

It was ten to nine when I heard a woman's voice in the waiting room.

"Will you put that away? I told you before not to play that here."

It was Jean's voice, and I smiled to myself as I imagined it was Peter who was playing some kind of game on his phone.

I finished the last line to a letter I was writing and went towards the door. It was just as I got there that I saw the outline shape of my secretary, Alice, on the other side of the glass partition. She knocked gently on the door, moments before I opened it and was able to greet her with a smile.

"I had a few things to do," I apologized.
I looked past Alice and saw Jean sitting on the sofa with a young man next to her. This, I realized, must be Peter. I moved forward to meet him.

"Hello, you must be Peter?" I said, as I introduced myself and held out my hand.

It was a small and nervous hand that took mine. But he was taller than I expected when he stood up.

"Hello, Jean. Glad to meet you again. Please come in."

I gestured toward the open door that led to my office and asked Alice for some drinks as I followed Peter and his mother inside.

As soon as we were all seated, I asked Peter if he liked playing computer games. He nodded quickly, then cast a glance at his mother and pulled himself back a little.

"I like them too," I said with a smile. It was not quite true, for I knew well the problems that these cause when the child becomes addicted to them and loses any sense of discipline they may have with their schoolwork. However, at this moment, the only important thing was to gain some happy acceptance from the boy as quickly as possible. Dealing with his obvious addiction to computer games could wait for another day.

As is normal for me, I seldom discuss the problem anyone has directly. I long ago found that anyone with a problem tends to expect this to be discussed, and so can close up. It's better to gain a degree of respect from each other. So it was that we spent a good part of the session talking about video games, football and the TV programs he likes. It was only once Peter began to relax and display a sense of familiarity that I asked him,

"Tell me, Peter, how do you feel about school?"

"It's OK," He responded, which of course, told me nothing.

"You're lucky," I laughed. "I hated Maths."

"Me too," He acknowledged with a grin.

"OK, can you show me how to do this algebra equation?" I asked, drawing a not very complex one on the pad I held over my knee.

Now, Peter was 15 at the time and should have had some understanding of Calculus. I have found that how quickly and how accurately an older student can do work at an elementary level, gives an indication of how familiar and so how successful they understand the subject matter. Peter did not do well. In fact, he got stuck very easily and seeing a tension build up in him, I quickly distracted him from the task.

"Would you feel happier if we swapped the X with a funny picture I asked and redrew the equation with a happy face instead of the X?" He grinned, and I felt the tension drain away.

Then I asked him, "Well, what would you like to substitute the X with?"

He shrugged his shoulders.
"Well, how about a P or a G?"

He looked puzzled.

"Can you do that?" He asked.

Then, I understood that Peter did not know what he was doing in trying to solve the equation. The X merely represents an unknown quality, and while he may have said he knew this, in reality, his mind did not understand how to manipulate the known factors to discover what the unknown one could be.

On realising Peter did not know the simple rules to work through an algebraic equation, I explained these to him, "First, you work out what is inside the brackets, then you do the multiplications and divisions, and finally the additions or subtractions," then, I told him a great secret, "Never ever, trust information. Check each line as you do it and then double-check your answer."

He smiled at me when I revealed this secret, for now, he found a reason to understand how he could get more sums correct. Peter did not have the nature to want to be top of the class. Rather, he just wanted everyone to be happy with him, and this he believed would be so if he got higher marks.

My real interest with Peter, of course, lay with his mother's concern that he was dyslexic. To investigate this, I asked Peter to write five lines of a story for me on a piece of paper I gave him. I told him he could write anything he wished. For with such a number of words, I can usually tell if a student understands how to construct a sentence, and so recognise spelling mistakes and verb tense usage. If not, I encourage them to expand to half or a full page.

Considering the fears of Jean, I was surprised to see a very reasonable presentation from Peter. There were very few mistakes in his grammar, and nothing I could see to warrant the suggestion that he was dyslexic. I, therefore, asked Peter if he would please join my secretary, and come back once he had written a full page completely by himself. I gave him a theme to choose from, and a few sub-goals to help him complete the page. As Peter left the room, I turned to Jean.

"Does Peter have a hearing problem?" I asked her because dyslexia is usually associated with mixing up vowels and this is often because the individual is or has developed to be poor in hearing the sound differences between, for example, 'a' and 'e'.

Jean shook her head and told me she had never noticed this. I decided to create some tests of my own to see how Peter could understand the difference between letters, although I had to acknowledge that there were no mistakes in the spelling of the words he had just written.

I asked his mother, why she had told me that Peter was dyslexic.

"It's only some times," she told me, "sometimes he can read everything and write very well, but other times he can't make sense of words. Sentences become confused and he struggles one day with pages that yesterday were clear and precise."

"Let us understand something Jean. The brain has two elements to process information. These are neurons and neurotransmitters. I spoke to you last time about this. Neurons are the pathways that allow signals to make sense with stored information in memory banks and suggest meanings. These do not move rapidly. They are held in a semi-permeable membrane that allows them some flexibility, but not enough to instantly destroy the pathways that have built up over time. Anyway, Peter shows that these networks are not destroyed, because it's only on certain occasions that the signal pathways appear to break down. This brings us to neurotransmitters, the chemicals that control how the signal moves between neurons. Now! While Peter is busy, I would like to explain something to you:

When some deep worry or fear disturbed our security in the past and we believe it may come again, we can create a ghost in our mind that haunts us. Children who have been abused and most certainly bullied can carry these ghosts, sometimes throughout their entire life.

Now, when we are frightened, our mind triggers a release of cortisol. This is a neurotransmitter. When the level of cortisol rises in the brain, it causes parts of the brain that deal with fast responses to be over-activated. It's very easy to understand this from a survival point of view.

When we are threatened, our brain needs to focus on how to deal with the threat. So, it closes down parts that would slow its response down. These are parts that deal with sensitive and rational thinking. At the same time, cortisol activates other parts that lead to muscle movement and so action. Our thinking, and so what we call intelligence, is largely dependent on other neurotransmitters. There are many of these, and you may have heard of dopamine, serotonin, and norepinephrine.

Basically, what happens is that when the mind is calm and interested, dopamine and serotonin, for instance, are conducting signals between neurons normally. The brain is in an optimum mode for learning. However, should the ghost of a bully come into the mind, cortisol will rise and this has the effect of lowering the activity of dopamine and serotonin. When this happens, the ability for learning falls as the mind is distracted. So, concentration drifts, parts become missed, and errors creep into existence through misunderstandings.

What I have just told you is not only what intelligence is about but it more precisely explains how and why students show different abilities in a lesson, as each lives through the stresses and strains of daily life.

The solution to improve learning dramatically in education would be to teach students how to meditate or at least accustom them to music that would create a balance between calmness and activation. This, in effect, would lower the level of cortisol, and so enable the other neurotransmitters to function at their normal level. However, too little of this is known in education, and if it is it's seldom practised."

I paused for a moment, and then added, "Now, while all this is as it is, let's see how this could apply to Peter's problem.

As you can understand, Jean, when Peter is relatively happy, his neurons conduct signals to other neurons because the chemicals or neurotransmitters function normally. However, something is triggering cortisol to take over. And, when it does, his brain goes into chaos. This creates great stress for him which further raises his cortisol level. The combined stress of all this creates panic in his mind, his visual system is affected, and his brain loses its ability to make sense of words. After a time, this trigger disappears from his mind, cortisol falls and the brain functions normally, so he can write the perfect composition he has just demonstrated. So, what we need to do is to find out what the trigger is."

"How do you think we can do this, Roy?"
"It requires first an understanding of what is happening, as I have just explained, and second, a method to bring it under control."
"How do you think we can do this?"

"Well, when Peter returns, I will explain all this to him in a way he will understand, so that he'll want to gain this control. Basically, we need to get him to write down any experience he feels that causes him to be nervous, and then to see if his problems with words soon show themselves. Where they do, we can begin to understand the root of his problem. Then, we need to teach him how to keep a perspective with this fear so that he can deal with it. This will be relatively easy enough. The real problem lies in identifying the trigger. Shall we call him back, and see how he has worked on the paper?"

So, it was that Peter returned with a perfectly acceptable essay, and I and his mother explained how he could begin to take control of his grades and so his life.

* *

In the months that unravelled before us, little sense seemed to be gained from the records that Peter kept. It seemed that there was no particular kind of incident that would trigger this confusion in his mind with words. What appeared to be a triggering incident one time did not disturb him at another. Yet, in another way, this led me to believe that it was not a particular incident itself that was causing the problem for Peter but some relationship with those that triggered great stress in him, which he had kept buried within his mind. As events unfolded, and unbeknown to his mother, Peter had been abused when he was younger. This trauma had not been released, and it was this that in seeking to find a way out of his subconscious was causing him to react to different incidents in different ways. Once this was understood and Peter could begin to deal with what had happened to him, he gradually began to try to take control of it.

Peter was not dyslexic. He was simply assumed to be so by the teachers and psychologists who were too ready to place him in a box. Their greater failure in all this was to believe that intelligence can be measured, that it can be related to an inherited gene, and then not to understand the difference between what IQ means and how intelligence comes to be, or for that matter what it is.

It was through understanding Peter's problem and those of many other human beings whom I have met, that I began to reject the easy classification of children, and indeed students of any age, on the restricted ability they displayed. As I came to realise, the belief that intelligence is inherited, even in some small way, is too quickly taken by many people to mean that performance in school can be related to a genetic quality. With this misunderstanding, it's reasoned that if a student appears to work hard but does not reach the standard expected, that their failing lies in their genes. The history behind this reasoning is very long, and yet it's full of bitter suspicion because of the political strategies from which it was born and those that continue to drive it, as we witnessed in 'The Bell Curve' published two decades ago.

This reasoning of inherited ability gives the teacher the right to hand out work, mark that work as it is returned, and so grade the student without themselves or the school they work for being shown to be accountable for this grade. The belief in inherited intelligence, large or small, is the only means by which education can justify the processing of its students.

My second book "Intelligence: The Great Lie" was written to explain exactly the influence of genetics in intelligence, and to put to rest all the misunderstandings that have arisen through the belief of nature vs nurture ratio. There simply is not one.

However, through this idea of processing children on their 'suspected inherited ability', came the idea that those who perform noticeably lower than others can be said to do so on an inherited basis. Once this became accepted, near paranoia spread throughout the teaching fraternity, such that once a child appeared to show any problems with reading or spelling, they were immediately branded 'genetically' dyslexic. Once a student was so branded, they are regarded as being different and treated as such, which makes them feel they will never be as good as other children, and this psychologically triggers off a whole host of behavioural and learning problems.

The same is so with a child who displays too much frustration and anger and is given a hat with ADHD stamped on the front.

The trouble here is that the role and purpose of the gene are completely misunderstood when it's believed to have such responsibility. The danger that comes out of this, is that while geneticists may be aware of such a gene (and this is arguable), the psychologists and teachers who learn of this readily assume that a gene coding has created the condition they witness.

However, the child's reading difficulty could have been caused by, as psychologists like to say, 'the environment' but let us suggest that the problem arises from some behavioural experience that was very disturbing to the child and that this altered the activity of chemicals in their brain. Such an instance would have no genetic cause. Yet, a situation would be created where the child is said to have a condition they do not, with all the obvious ramifications that develop from this.

There again, let's suppose the child did inherit a gene for dyslexia (and it would take a geneticist in a special laboratory and not a psychologist working with theories to identify if this was so), there is absolutely no way of knowing if that gene is active or dormant. If it is active, the interaction it makes with proteins could negate the effect it's supposed to give. On the other hand, if it's dormant, it will have absolutely no role in the genetic makeup of this individual. In a sense, it won't be there.

Now the problem, as we understand it, is that teachers, psychologists, and parents hear of a gene causing dyslexia, so the moment a child struggles more than others in reading or spelling the cause is thought to be genetic, after which they are readily labelled dyslexic. Once this happens, the child is either left to remain in the class, where the teacher seldom knows or has the time to really help them, or they are isolated from other children and given special help which makes all aware that they are different.

As we can understand, if they are removed from their peers to be given special treatment, this will deprive them of developing normal social skills. Not only will this hinder the development of their intelligence, because they are not developing their ability to know how to adapt their emotions with others (which can interfere with their awareness in learning), but it also means that the environment they are placed in will most likely feed the condition they have.

On the other hand, if they are left in the class with their peers, they will either drift along at their own rate (because the teacher does not have the time to give them more help than other students), or the teacher will let them 'learn by themselves', fearful of pushing them beyond what they suspect they are actually capable of. Both of these create the limiting world that prevents the child from learning how to overcome this difficulty they have.

What needs to be realized from this is that even if a child does have a gene that coincides with the condition that several children display, there is no evidence that their gene arrangement is in anyway responsible for their condition. Such a condition can have been totally created through environmental circumstances, and could, therefore, be one that the child could be educated out of by a sensitive and knowledgeable teacher, as I have illustrated here with Peter.

Without an understanding of this, which is why I discussed Peter here and will shortly do so with Mathew, psychologists try to raise ability through endlessly simulative tasks and use unfathomable equations to explain their findings, when all they really needed was to give love because it is love that opens up empathy to try to understand the world that the mind of another has grown through. Intelligence I found, really comes from the heart, because it is foremost an emotionally based means of evaluation. As we have found with Peter, all the networks of his brain that could easily produce the finest example of a written composition for his age were completely devastated, every time his heart bled.

Chapter Five
Mathew

The phone buzzed in my pocket, just as I was getting into my car.

"Can you help me please?" It was a woman's voice and she sounded much stressed.

"I'll try. What's the matter?"

"My son might get expelled!" The voice sounded both angry and desperate at the same time.

"What has happened?" I tried to sound calm to soothe her.

"The little bugger has just set the fire extinguisher off! It shot down the corridor like a torpedo. Thank God no one was hurt."

And so, this was how I came to meet Mathew.

Mathew was a little bit older than Peter, and I remember how he impressed me with the way he explained his mind when he came into my office. He introduced himself very politely, and with a clear manner of confidence.

As soon as we exchanged formalities, he began immediately to inquire into my life and experiences. He wanted to know the countries I had been to, and what I thought about this and about that. He was very well versed in current events. The image he projected was of a confident and very able young man. However, as soon as he picked up a pen to write the short essay I had asked of him, the whole character of Mathew changed. It was like watching a Jekyll and Hyde movie, except that instead of becoming a monster the young man in front of me was transformed into a highly nervous and much stressed human being.

As I watched Mathew write, it was not the badly formed words that drew my attention but the grip with which he held the pen. As I watched white patches on the surface of his skin appear with the pressure he applied, it was highly interesting for me to see how letters appeared with no conformity. One letter could be twice the size of the one it followed and selected from a different model to the one it would precede.

Watching the stress build up in this young man as he struggled in the task of writing, I noticed how the end letters to a word would be hastily scribbled as he urgently strove to conclude it. So, each word would begin clearly but by the end, it would be illegible. His parents had been told he had a motor tremor and would always be like this. There was nothing that could be done, they were told. His mother had told me how he was the problem child in a class, the burden of every teacher.

It was, in fact, because of Mathew's problem with writing that his mother had thought to meet me. The incident with the fire extinguisher had caused her to take action before things got more out of control.

I did not focus my interest on his class behaviour. I understood that his resistance to the system that limited him was obviously a tactic to explain his poor performance as an act of self-defiance, rather than one of inadequacy. Yet, what did stir my interest was the cause of this inadequacy?

I had listened to the explanation of his motor tremor but had noticed that this tremor only occurred towards the end of a word, and was, therefore, in some way related to a meaning of stress. This aside, I had witnessed how he demonstrated a high degree of finger dexterity in various games and tasks I had seen him involved with. Putting this tremor explanation aside, I began to study how he held a pen and applied it to the paper I had given him.

Now, if I were to ask you to pick up a pen with your eyes closed, you would feel for the correct position of the pen within your fingers, and make adjustment until it was right for you. Each of us has our own way of holding and making use of a pen. When this young man held a pen, it was so close to the tip that he retarded any operation of dexterity that he might make in forming a letter. I asked him to try to accept a different hold upon the pen he was using, and while such new positioning was unnatural for him, he was more able to elaborate on the description of a character. Why I pondered should the form of letters be so inconsistent?

When the child begins school for the first time, they are taught 'rules' by which they can learn to do things. So, they learn how to set a book correctly on their desk, how to hold a pencil and how to write letters, etc. As a class of children are thus indoctrinated, some will watch the teacher and others will watch and copy from those next to them. All will be eager to show the teacher they have finished first.

In such a way, the infant will learn to compartmentalise the paper they have been given into potential lines and spaces. As they decide where the left-hand margin will be, so they decide where the right-hand one will lie, and so the point at which their writing will move to a lower line.

If the paper has no lines, so they will learn how to write across the page by constantly referring to past letters, marks higher up the page, and the potential space to the right, so that the line of their writing is even and balanced. When the paper is marked into lines, as it more often is, they will learn to create an imaginary line that sets the height of lowercase letters, such that the 'a's, 'e's, 'i's and 'o's etc. look level. In this way, the letters of the words will appear uniform, when they rest on the bottom line. This writing may seem automatic, but it is learned through such rules.

So, with experience, the child automatically and now naturally scans for the height and the width of each character before they make it. With every act of performance, no matter how small or how irrelevant it may seem to be, it had to be learned at one time. That learning required a degree of sensitivity in how to perform the actions of another person, as they learned from them.

In the same way that you may verbally talk to yourself when you learn to change gears in a car for the first time, and then no longer need to do this as you progressed to automatically perform this action, so the child in school is minutely conscious of small details when they first learn a task.

You only have to watch an infant watch the one they are sitting next to, to see how they watch and mimic their actions as they pick up a pencil and write a letter. They will see how the pencil is held, and they will examine what the letter looks like that has been drawn. Then, they will draw their personalised version of this, as they constantly check how it compares as they give it shape.

So, while we think about the words we are to write, we must remember that we learned to know that when 'a' followed 'i' that it was to be kept at the same height, while an 'l', 't', or 'h' was to be taken to twice this height. Therefore, our mind constantly seeks reference points, where it searches backwards and forwards to know how to adjust the size and form of each new character to make such a uniform presentation. This is something that we learn to do, and like riding a bicycle we are not normally aware of how we do this. We just do it. Nevertheless, it's a learned operation based upon rules.

However, this 16-year-old did not know these rules! He did not see how one letter needed to be related to the one it followed, just as this would set the stage for those to come. The question in my mind was 'Why did he not see this?'

As we worked together to learn this skill, Mathew explained to me how he had been taunted for being fat when he first began school, and how he hated to be in that class because he was always picked on by the other children. When I met him he was not so, but I could understand from the way he explained his feelings that the first years of school life had been quite traumatic for him.

Knowing of this brought sense to why he had hated to be in school earlier in his life, and so why he tried everything he could think of to escape from it. When others took note of the scale of letters, his mind was on other thoughts. In being so distracted, he only half noticed what others took more note of, and this caused him to take less care and be less aware of what was happening. As time went by, the inability he showed to make such a uniform presentation became more and more accepted as 'his' way.

So, while Mathew was in primary school much of what he was taught, the basic rules to understand how to comply with the academic world fell on deaf ears. He so much hated to be in his classroom that he could not focus on his learning, and so developed a very bad structure to engage information. Perhaps, considering the complexity of the human mind he may have done this purposely, simply to demonstrate his rejection of a world that gave him pain.

Eventually, with all this understood, we discussed rules of character formation and relationships. By making a small mark at the appropriate height in between the inked lines on the right side of the paper, he learned to devise an imaginary line that extended from the letters on the left, so that he could define a particular size for each letter he was about to write. Within less than an hour of practice, he had written 'abcde' in joined-up writing with a precision that was remarkable. Not that this was easy but at 16 he had much to relearn.

The important point was that Mathew discovered that he could do this, and he began to learn how to do it better. The explanation for his very distinctive change in performance came not simply through someone showing him how to do something, but because of the quality of language shared between the teacher and the taught that enabled the psychology to change the physiology. (We discussed the great importance of this in earlier books.) While his limitation, and the placing this had given him in the class, had always been thought to be genetic, it was proven to be purely environmental. Mathew did not have dyslexia, and once he discovered that he could join the system and be as good as anyone else, he stopped fighting it.

Mathew's story shows how small misunderstandings that are passed over when they occur, can so easily cause teachers of a later time to regard the performance they witness as more innate than developed. Once this belief takes hold, the teacher can so easily feel that the student's real development is beyond the time and energy they have.

With a better understanding now of how the insecurity of the mind can develop poor networks of relationships in the brain, let us return to Peter.

\

Chapter Six
"Why Did They Say That About My Son?"

It was raining heavily outside, and Peter's mother had just entered the room. It had been two weeks now since I had first met Peter and his mother's apparent freedom from the worry that had haunted her was a welcome sight. I helped her to take her wet coat off and hung it on the old coat stand I had bought in an antique shop. Coats hang much better on it, whereas coats piled up on top of one another on a coat rack fastened to the wall never look the same.

"I wanted to ask you," she began as soon as she was seated before me, "can you explain to me why Peter's teachers thought he was dyslexic? I see a real change in him now. He is keeping a record of things that stress him. He really understands how he can control his own grades now."

"Sometimes the question is very easy to ask, Jean, but the answer can be very long."

"Do you have time, please? I would really like to know. It has been puzzling me since you first began to explain how Peter understands his world."

I went over to the door and asked Alice to bring in two coffees this time. I needed mine black, and with the sugar that my girlfriend so wisely tells me is very unhealthy, "It's a killer!" She keeps telling me.

As I eased myself back in my chair, I looked at the woman in front of me. She had changed so much from the first time I met her. Like her son, she had found something to believe in, something she could learn to control. She understood there were no certainties, but at least she found out how she could be involved in a constructive way to help Peter.

"The problem," I began, "is that we don't really know how the mind of each child works. It's not just that the teachers think that intelligence is inherited in some way and so feel that some child with a big problem is beyond them because of this, but also because they don't have the time to really think about each child in their class. It's not easy with 30 kids to understand how the mind of each works when you only have 45 minutes, and won't see them again for maybe a week. In time, the teacher will get a feel for how each student responds, but this does not show why they respond in the way they do, and without knowing this, they have no real understanding of how to begin to make the change they would like to see.

As I mentioned to you when we first met, school is a processing system of a processing society. It has been this way since the need for a general education first came to be. We don't like to think it is or to believe it is like this because we love children and want to believe that each will get the best opportunity they can in school for the life they will live.

But you only have to see how infants of five or six years old are herded into a classroom, told to copy things and reproduce them, and then see how different coloured stars are given out. As the emotions of each child allows them to concentrate, and by the ways other children behave towards them, so each will learn skills in how to deal with information and how to know how to present it.

Now, how they present their mind to another is very important. Those who have been raised to do this well, are usually the ones who adapt better in school and learn how to give information the way the teacher wants it."

I noticed the door open, and Alice comes in with two steaming mugs. It was a welcome sign for me to pause for a moment, and for Jean to drink something hot.

"Don't they all learn that way?" She asked, after taking a sip.

I smiled a little. "Lots of kids when ask a question, just shrug and say 'I don't know'!"

Jean gave a slight 'um' sound as she nodded in understanding.

"Well, of course, they know something, but they were not raised at home or not tutored in school to know how to explain their thoughts better. So, they just switch off. It would be better if we raised children to respond with 'I'm not sure if I know'."

"Does that make a difference?"

"A very big one," I replied, "The 'I don't know' is final. It ends the interaction. But the 'I'm not sure if I know' encourages it. This causes the teacher to ask why, and from these distracting thoughts emerge those that can be moulded to give a sense of understanding. It's a very big difference.

"Then, why don't teachers correct children?"

This time, I smiled to myself.

"You have to imagine the teacher asking a class a question. They may choose one student, and if that student says 'I don't know' what is the teacher to do? Do they move to the next to keep all minds engaged, or do they concentrate on this one student and risk the whole class being bored and losing control?"

"Can't they help just a little?"

"Exactly, the teacher needs to create a change in the mindset of their class. When they first meet the class, they need to explain the difference between 'I don't know' and 'I'm not sure if I know', and then encourage the students to question themselves and what they are doing more often. If they can learn to do this, they would more likely respond with a higher level of interaction when they are asked a question because their mind would be working more with information."

"You make it sound as if we teach children to be stupid."

I pulled back from Jean.

"In a sense, Jean, education has been doing this since it was first created."

"How?" She looked puzzled.

"By not teaching children how to think and by accepting them in the ways they have developed to do this from their parents and the narrow world in which they live."

I took a drink of coffee. It was quickly going cold. I talk too much, my children tell me.

"Look," I explained further, "You can go into a class of students of any age and if you took the time to deeply examine their knowledge of a question, you would find that most of them could answer it. You would also notice that each will have developed a skill in language to explain their mind in their own way. It's just a skill in language." I gave a slight shrug to express the point.

"But this 'skill'," – I said with emphasis – "is what makes much of the difference in the grades they get. So, it's those who learned a long time ago how to present their mind in the right way, that will get the higher marks."

Jean was watching me very closely now. I could see her thinking of how she could explain this to Peter.

I anticipated the question I saw forming in her mind.
"It begins, as all things do, in infancy," I told her, "parents who tell more stories to their child, parents who build up their child's vocabulary through interaction…"

"What do you mean interaction?" She interrupted me.

"Well, don't just read a story but engage the child's mind in the story. Interrupt it in parts. Ask them what they think about something, and what they think may happen next. Then, as they grow older, help them to engage the thoughts of very many different people. The more experience they have of life (you can say streetwise), the more they will know how to reach the mind and feelings of another. This is the skill in a language I have talked about before.

Then, once they get into school, you need to find out the rules by which the 'school mind' works, and teach these to your child. Remember, school life is based on rules; when to do this, when to do that, and how to do it. If you teach your child to be aware of these rules then they can learn to play the game. It is, of course, the game of life, learning to understand the hopes and expectations of others. The faster you adapt, the smoother things go."

Jean nodded. All this was new and interesting for her. She had never thought of school this way.

"But this," I said, as I reached over and moved some papers aside, "brings us back to why a school processes children and does not teach them more individually."

"How could it teach them more individually? I mean could they have smaller classes?"

"That would be wonderful, but it's not realistic. It would cost too much money. No, the ways students could be taught more individually would be to teach them how to think better. Teach them reasoning skills from day one. Give them the tools to take more control over their learning process."

"How?" She held a puzzled look.

"Well, as the parent teaches their child to be aware of the world, so the school teacher could do the same. They could teach them rules of awareness and how to process information sensitively. The mind does not just remember things. The brain has built up its own way of processing and storing information. So, we could teach children how to improve their memory."

"What? You mean like showing them things, hiding them and asking what they can remember."

"That would be one way, and this would develop their skill of awareness and this sensitivity, but there are many ways; Mnemonics, for example, learning strategies to store information into categories would be another."

"But," she interrupted again, "different children will be different. Some will be faster than others."

"Ah! Some will have developed to be faster than others," I corrected her, "But there is nothing stopping the slowest to build up their speed. They just need to learn to concentrate, anticipate and practise their reactions. I remember in my youth the boxer, Muhammad Ali. He had the fastest reaction time of anyone on the planet, but he was not born that way. He trained himself to be the fastest. Thinking, like anything else, is something we learn to do. By thinking more about how we think, like making different strategies and practising the skills involved with these, we can learn to think better, and," I added, "faster."

"This seems very easy," Jean relaxed back in her chair. "So, why don't teachers do this?"

"Perhaps, some do. But they have a lesson schedule to keep."

"No, I mean why don't they all teach this?"

"Ah! You mean like a subject," I smiled again. "Well that, Jean, would take us back to why school today still produces a citizen of a bygone age. The citizen of the 19th and 20th Centuries was never meant to think, well at least not too much. So, children in school were not…" I corrected myself, "…are not taught this way."

"Mind you," my thoughts drifted for a moment trying to find a simple way to explain this, "…well, you see, a long time ago, there were only religious schools. The purpose of these was to raise children to be morally good citizens. This was the time of the agricultural era, when most people worked in fields or were apprenticed to a trade, so only a very basic education was provided to most children.

However, when we moved into the industrial phase of our civilisation and things became a little bit technical, children needed to be taught to be ready for the work skills necessary for them as adults. So, the school began to formally teach them reading, writing and arithmetic, the 3 Rs, plus other subjects to fill out the week such as geography and science. Oh, and don't forget the subject of religious studies, because the real purpose of the school was to teach children moral skills and good ethics. Well, at least it was until we hit the 1970s and there was a big change in politics. After this, schools tried not to interfere in the ways the parents want their children to be raised, and so moral guidance in school began to fade away."

"And with it, the discipline in the classroom," Jean added.

I nodded. "True. Before this, discipline was kept with the teacher using a cane, but once this became illegal many teachers did not and do not know how to keep discipline in the class. So, they shout, get stressed, the children know how to play on this, and the whole thing goes more out of control. What is needed is for teachers to learn how to reach the hearts of their students."

"How would they do this?"

"Love, of course. Learning how to tell a story is a very good way to create a bond of trust and understanding."

"Really?"

"We all love stories. They give information in a way that let us find our own identity in them. We all love people who can tell a good story. Students in school are no different...Anyway," I continued, trying to keep our conversation on track, "the education that came to be in the industrial era had a purpose. This was to identify which children would be the managers or controllers in the future, and which would be the workers. What the society did not want were citizens who reasoned too much.

Remember that the 19th Century saw the birth of socialism. This was an era of great political change, and those at the top of the social order became increasingly nervous of a revolution erupting that would remove them from power. We don't think like this today, but they certainly did in the 19th Century. So, the requirement of school was to produce a general citizen who could reason just enough to do their job efficiently, but not to think too much on the ways the world worked and so how they were governed."

"Well! How do you stop people from thinking?"

"You can't! But you can teach them to think in simple terms. Yes, or No, and not to question. And this is what school did. It only taught children to think in yes or no terms. We call this dualistic thinking. The thing is that nothing has changed. Schools today, in 2024, still teach children in this way of thinking."

Jean's eyes widened, "Really?" she exclaimed.

I could see from the expression on her face that she was struggling with a thought.

"So, where do the managers come from?" she asked.

"Well, the children who were raised by parents to be more aware of the importance of understanding information did better in school, and they were the ones who usually went to university. You see, it's in university that students are really taught how to think, question, analyze and evaluate. Those who manage to get into this level of education are turned into the future managers."

"But children from poor backgrounds could learn these skills you talk about and could get into university."

"Ah, yes! But you see education at this level was not to be free. It cost a lot of money to have this level of education. So, basically, it was rich parents who better prepared their children in how they thought and also could afford to send them to university, and often to private schools that better prepared them for this opportunity."

"How could a private school do this?" Jean was now very interested in the whole and very unfair mechanism behind the school.

"Look at what happens in a state school," I began to explain, "Most children have poor self-discipline, come from homes where they received little development in concentration, so their minds easily wander. They have low mental stamina and so give up easily with a problem because they don't know the rules to get through it and they tend to be insecure so they try to intimidate each other. Their classes will have some 30 or 40 students and so their teachers will have really no time to help each student understand really what they are trying to learn. Basically, they are left to get on with it themselves. When school is over at three-thirty they go home, play computer games, eat dinner, watch mindless television programs and finally fall asleep way past a good bedtime.

Now! Compare this child to one who was raised by parents with a good academic background. They will have been taught to read and write, and know some arithmetic before they began school. They will have been raised to think in the languages of school and so be more familiar with it when they get there. They will know some of the rules of the languages of English, or Chinese or Arabic or whatever their national language is, and the rules of mathematics.

Their competence in these two languages will really decide how well they do in school because the school does not work on intelligence it works on language and emotional stability. Their class will have 20 or 25 students in. This really does make a huge difference. It gives the teacher some real-time to be with each student and so give each the personal help they need when they get stuck. Now, when their school day finishes, they will have extra lessons at home and when they get home, their parents will likely share time with them discussing the events of the day and give them a purpose to all this. They will be encouraged to think of being a lawyer, doctor, and accountant and so have a purpose to study when they are in school."

Jean looked down into her near-empty mug, "I didn't think of school like this. I thought it was just for children to learn."

"Everything is politics Jean, everything."

"So, why don't we teach children how to think today? I mean we now have equal rights in education."

"You would have to read my book 'The Illusion of Education' and the other books I have written to really understand this. But in a nutshell, it's because we believe that intelligence is inherited. And, as I explained to you when we first met, even though we can never know the genetic worth of an individual's intelligence when teachers and psychologists can't find a way to raise the performance ability of a student, they automatically assume this is because of how they were born. When they find 'human beings' like this," I emphasised the word 'human beings' because I wanted to demonstrate how individual we are and so cannot be understood in a collective manner, "they put them in a box called dyslexia or ADHD and so on."

"This is what they did to my son."

I nodded. "It happened to me too...! When I was 16, I was told I would never be able to learn mathematics and was put into a low-level class that was only taught arithmetic. When I came to leave school and took my final examinations, I completely failed this. But this classification was wrong. I mean it was right when the teachers looked at my performance, but nobody tried or had the time to help me to change that performance. I was just, well processed."

"Really?" she looked a little taken aback.

I nodded. "It was only when I stopped trusting the school, learned to think for myself, and was guided by a very kind teacher who knew what he was doing, that I was able to pass the subject of formal mathematics a few years later, at a very high, pre-university level and with the very highest distinction."

"I am really beginning to understand what you mean now about how we process our children. I just trusted the teachers to help Peter as best they could."

"Oh, don't get me wrong. Some would have really worried about how to help your son. The problem is not so much the individual teacher but the ways they are trained: like thinking intelligence is inherited and by the ways they are conditioned to work. They have only minutes, really, and these are stressful minutes to share their mind and to decide how to give out marks."

"What do you mean?"

"Well, this processing system has really one aim. It's to offer a range of skills to the working world. So, as infants are awarded gold, silver and blue stars, and older children 9/10 and 6/10 in their class and homework marks, all these are conditioning ways to the grades they will gain when they finally leave school. These grades decide, of course, who will be allowed to become 'the butcher, the baker and the candlestick maker."

"Rub-a-dub-dub," she laughed a little remembering the children's verse, but then became more serious as she realized I meant professionals, trade, and unskilled workers.

I nodded, as I read her thoughts. She was smart, and so was her son, I reminded myself.

Jean looked a little blown out by the simplicity of the whole error by which school works. As she sat there finishing her coffee, I could understand the many questions that were rising to the surface in her thoughts. Sure enough, she looked up to me and said,

"When did we start to classify children by dyslexia?"

"Well, It was only given official recognition towards the end of the last century, but the mind-frame to group individuals by the condition or ability they display goes back a long time."
I could see that Jean was interested to hear more.

"This needs to classify and so box ability grew out of the efforts of an early psychologist in America, by the name of Henry

Goddard. In fact, Goddard was the first person to create an intelligence test in America. Well, actually, he corrupted a French way of understanding the reason for children having very poor learning abilities, into a way of selecting would be desirables in the American immigration process.

But it was Goddard who invented the term 'moron' to identify feebleminded people. Through this classification over 100,000 human beings who displayed signs of feeblemindedness or were said to be insane, diseased, or born criminals and even those who were blind, deaf or deformed, were compulsorily sterilised against their will."

"Why?" Jean looked shocked.

"To prevent them from having children, and so, reducing the likelihood of this condition of feeblemindedness in the American society," I shrugged my shoulders, "It was a cleansing policy."

She looked horrified.

"Well, it still continues today in some countries. But the thing is that Goddard made up this idea of feeblemindedness. Genetically, there was nothing wrong with these people. They had just had a very poor development and so exhibited a very low learning ability. All of these people could have been developed to function normally. I wrote a lot about this in 'The Hidden Secrets of Intelligence Revealed'. Simply, we do not understand what human intelligence is when we classify human beings into boxes."

She looked at me for a moment. "You just mentioned ADHD, what is that?"

"ADHD means attention deficit hyperactivity disorder. It's a name given to kids who are hyperactive. So, when a child has too much energy and this is linked to bad behaviour, they are readily now said to have ADHD and given a drug like Ritalin to calm them down. In a way, this is linked to dyslexia because if the child can't concentrate in their lessons because of their high activity, they will miss rules that help them to understand how to spell, read etc."

"You mean they give children drugs in school?"

I nodded my head slowly. "Often compulsorily. If the parent's refuse to have the drug given to their child they can be expelled from the school. Ritalin is prescribed by doctors to some twelve percent of children in American schools today, and yet we don't have any clue to the possible long-term side effects of it."

"Side effects!" the expression on Jean's face was a mixed one of shock and concern.

"When you put any chemical in the body, it reacts with the body in more than one way."

"Look!" I explained to her, "children on Ritalin commonly have anxiety problems. They are nervous and agitated easily. They can't sleep at night-time. They can vomit, have headaches, feel dizzy, experience loss of appetite, and have skin rashes, nerve disturbances such as numbness and tingling, stomach pains…"

"Woah! Woah! Stop there. Are you serious?"

"Very serious, and as I said, we do not know how all this will affect them in 20 or 30 years time."

Jean looked pale, "I had no idea," she said.

"So, what would you now say if I told you that an increasing number of neurologists, those who understand how the brain works, are beginning to agree that there is no such thing as ADHD?"[5 / 6]

If Jean had been holding her cup at that time, she would have dropped it. So clear was the look on her face.

I nodded again.

"A new and very major study emerged in 2016, explaining that this hyperactivity in children is a result of stress in their lives. One explanation lies in the frustration some children feel when they are pushed to compete with older children."[7]

"What do you mean older. They are all in the same class, aren't they?"

"A child is placed in a class not by their actual age, but on the date they were born which fits in with the school year. There is a huge difference in the ability of the brain and so of the mind with children a year in difference. So, you find a child who is seven, struggling to keep up with a whole class of eight-year-olds. Without understanding this, teachers see a younger child in their class behaving strangely, not able to concentrate as well as others, have a short attention span, are restless and constantly fidgeting, etc. Then, they witness explosions of frustration and that's it! The child is rubber-stamped as having ADHD, rushed to the school psychologist, then to the doctor and most likely placed on medication."

"This is really scary."

"Well, it's happening to thousands of children around the world, simply because we don't stop and try to understand the mind of the human being. Like I said before, school is a processing system all too ready to classify and grade on appearances."

"Do they have to use drugs?"

"Well, this comes back to the misunderstanding about the inheritance we have. You see ADHD is said to run in families and this is taken by far too many to say it's genetic. But ADHD is only 'new'. No one knew about it 50 years ago. We say it runs in families, but this might just mean the parents and not the grandparents or even those further back. The problem can too often be just too much sugar. It is really disturbing how obese our children are becoming because we pump them with too much sugar. It is this sugar, which is highly addictive, that is too often behind the spiralling incidents we have of ADHD now, but of course, there are other factors. Yet, instead of controlling diets, we just pump kids with drugs. It's the quick and easy way. Besides, to run in families does not have to mean it is genetic."

"What else could it be?"

"Socially inherited; simply copying."

"What do you mean socially inherited?"

"Take schizophrenia for instance. We now know that if a parent is schizophrenic, then their behaviour can affect the way their child learns to react to their world. This is not just mental copying, but the impressions the child's mind gains from the behaviour of their parent can change their brain chemistry. So, they become schizophrenic!

In the same way, the signs of ADHD, such as emotional outrage and displays of frustration, can be a language that children have seen and believe is correct to mimic. In this way, such a condition can be passed through a family purely by influence and have nothing to do with genes.[8] Once you really start to understand how genes work, you realise that nothing is black and white."

I paused for a moment and felt a smile of recognition come to my face.

"When I wrote a chapter on genetics in a book, I gave it the title 'A riddle wrapped in a mystery inside an enigma'."

"That sounds confusing."

"Exactly the point, Jean," then added, "the environment that feeds the gene is far, far more complex than most imagine."

"Such as?"

"Well, look at ADHD. I recall a study in 2014 that explained how it can develop in a child if their mother took Tylenol when she was pregnant. But there again, it's now reasoned that this condition can develop if the newborn is deprived of immediate contact with its mother for too long a period. If it is, the processing systems of their brain can relate too much to inanimate structures instead of facial recognition procedures, which are essential at that age for sound emotional development.[9] This would explain why ADHD children have difficulty to relate to and so express feelings, and that with frustration for this they tend to explode in outbursts. The afterbirth environment of the child is far, far more complex than we take it to be."

"This is amazing."

"Well, no, it isn't. It just means that we have lost the ability to consider more how any feature of the human being develops. Or

(And this is perhaps more true), we don't take the time to think more about it. We just see something and accept it for what it is, exactly the same with intelligence."

"But doesn't the IQ test measure a child's intelligence? I was reading about it."

"It's a fallacy. I have explained how this idea arose and why it was politically marketed."

Jean tried to look convinced.

"It's a mindset that has been created, just like the one that the whole world believed in 500 years ago."

Her eyes darted but looked nowhere, as if to find what I meant in her mind.

"That the world is flat," I helped her.

"The whole idea that you can measure the individual intelligence of a human being is wrong. Look, from a genetic viewpoint and most psychologists know nothing about genetics; it's impossible to go from the population level to the individual."

"What does that mean?" She interrupted me.

"Well, the belief is quite false that you can take a group of people and examine similarities within them, and see how these are different to those of another group of people. When you look at the individuals within any group, there is nothing identical in their personal environments that give you anything to judge the role of the gene by. In fact," I said rather forcefully, "we are now realising that we don't know enough about the gene in the first place."

"But I heard we had discovered all the genes."

"True. We know that the human being is made up of 23,000 genes (although more recent suggestions double this), but this does not tell us how those genes work and how they react with each other. Human genetics is not the same as plant genetics. How can you measure a feeling or a dream?"

I smiled to myself, thinking of a drawing I had once seen of a teacher pouring 'information' from a watering can into the empty heads of different children in a class, to show that different heads could hold different amounts. It tied in with what people think of genetic ability, which is, of course, totally wrong.

"Remember," I added, "even knowing about a gene gives no explanation as to how its purpose unfolds at any particular moment, after all the proteins it manufactures to carry its instruction are dependent upon the chemicals available in the cell at that precise moment, and these change every instant, especially once emotion comes into the picture. You can see this very easily if you think of bullying.

Let's say that a child is born with a great genetic ability to learn. We can't say this, but just let's pretend for the sake of argument. Now, they seem to learn very quickly in infancy. They go to school and are happy for the first year. In the second year, other children start to pick on them for some reason. Maybe they wear glasses, or their parents can't afford better clothes.

Whatever the reason, they feel emotionally hurt; they lose confidence to explain the thoughts they have to others. Once this begins, they lose the ability to define information sensitively when they encounter it. As information is vaguely registered, so it's vaguely stored. This means that their memory is poorly organised. This means that they become less able to associate with what is happening, to what they understood in the past, and so don't recognise what information means as they used to do.

Now, if this rejection from others in their class continues they will play to what is expected of them, even though they most likely are unaware of doing this. This is a very normal human thing to do for survival. Many years later, the child who was born with a great ability does poorly in school and leaves with low grades in their final examinations.

This, of course, is a very simple illustration, but if you magnify that little bullying and realise that every child develops through a circus of acceptance and rejection, of love and abuse from their parents, friends, school children and teachers, after all, not all teachers are loving or have the time for their emotional needs, nor do they know how to reach the heart of their students when they try to teach them; you can begin to understand that intelligence is a myriad of complexities that are far, far too unfathomable to ever measure. The belief that it could arise so that children could be simply, and I mean very simply, processed through their school years.

If this were not so, education could not have functioned at the time when the teacher was given 50 or even 100 students in their class. Of course, they only have about 30 in a class now, but this is still too large a number when the teacher and the parents together do not understand the real role they play in the development of those children. Mind you," – I held my mug up to Jean – "the bigger problem is that children don't understand why they have to go to school in the first place."

"I never did."

"Exactly the point, me too. I never understood why I had to go to school every day of my childhood. It was just something that was forced upon me, and when I was there I was never happy. I had no idea what was going on in my life. It was only when my daughter began school that I began to realise what was happening, and that was too many years too late for me. Anyway, as each child finds their own purpose, so each will make their effort." I called Alice and asked if we could have two more coffees.

"Should I have pushed Peter harder when he was younger?" "Oh, that is an extremely difficult question to answer. I have met students who had long lost interest because their parents, and usually the father, pushed them too hard. Perhaps, they realized how important school is and wanted their child not to waste this opportunity. But the human mind is not a machine. Knowing how much push to give and how much not to give is a very difficult balance. You really need to understand the mind of the child. The problem is that parents tend to see what they want to see, and don't always realise the damage they do. Very few parents actually know how the mind of their child really works. They know how they behave, but knowing what the mind is really seeking is not the same thing."

"I saw that with the way my brother pushed his son. William just gave up."

"I remember a father asking me why his daughter was not doing well in her school work. I met the child and realized she had lost the inner drive. Her father had said too many times that she must work hard. It killed the spirit inside her. There was no fun to learn. So, I told the father to look at a large plant that was placed in the room in which we sat. As he did so, I asked him to imagine how the plant needs the carbon dioxide we breathe out and how it needs nitrogen in the soil to grow, but most importantly, it needs love to be vibrant in its life.

I related experiments where people did give love to plants and how they grew so much differently through this. I don't think I can ever forget the look on the face of the father and how he said to me 'Now I understand' It is difficult to know how much to push and how much to guide. Some get it right and others... Well," – I lifted my shoulders to emphasise the point – "All the child wants to do is just to be happy."

"That's what we all want."

"It's true," I had to agree with her, but felt I had to add, "If we thought more about being kinder to others in our actions and thoughts, we would create that happier world for ourselves."

"You mean, keep your mouth shut."

I could not resist a sharp laugh, "Well, I think we could all do with thinking before we say something at times!"

I remembered, at that point, the problem that was emerging from Peter, and changed the direction the conversation was going.

"Emotion really is the key to good schoolwork and so success with grades, you know."

"You mean to be happy."

"Well, happiness is a transient thing. Sometimes, we need to be a bit unhappy to know when we are really happy. No, I mean a sense of peace inside. It is this that really allows the mind to be sensitive to the world about it, and it is this that drives the wiring of the brain to build up the better neural connections," I glanced at her face to make sure she was following me, before continuing.

"So, when the child (Well actually we need to say the student now because this is a lifelong process) has that quality of peace mixed with a fascination to explore, then we have the ideal learning condition. Then, they are sensitive to the world about them, identify with it better and so build up more accurate memory banks which they can better access later on. Any child, rather any human being can have this quality, but each, of course, develops in the world that is created for them by others."

"You mean the parents."

"Initially yes, when they are an infant. But by the first six months, the baby will already have begun to take notice of the attitude, emotions and interests of those about them. So, we can then extend this to family members, childhood friends and once they attend social organisations, which, of course, are kindergarten and then primary school, the mixed egos, needs, desires and struggling identities that will help or injure them as their personality and drives are moulded.

You know, the parents and teachers should really work together much more than they do. It's such a big problem when parents thinks the education of their child is just up to the teacher."

"You mean if I had worked closely with the teachers, and if they had worked closely with me, we could have helped Peter more?"

"Well, let's think of the future," I replied, "We have something to work on now, and Peter can still catch up. The most important thing is that he knows it."

Jean looked at me for a long time. I could see thoughts taking shape.

"All that you say is totally new to me. I really never thought of what my son was going through in school. I just wanted to know that he was happy, no one was bullying him and the teachers would say good things in the parent's evenings," She thought more for a moment after saying this as if struggling to know how to add something.

"I have mentioned you to my friend. I hope you wouldn't mind, and well," Jean struggled further to find words or perhaps feelings she wanted to share, "and well…she told other women in her work. We kind of wondered if you, well, if you would have the time to meet a group of mothers and tell them how to raise their children?"

"Oh, I can't do that. Every parent must learn to listen to their own heart. But I would love to meet both mothers and fathers one evening, and talk to them about some things they may not yet have realized in developing the ability of their child in school. Yes! Let's do it!" I felt so happy to be meeting other parents.

Chapter Seven
I Meet the Parents

It was nearly three weeks later before I pulled up outside the village hall, where I was to meet Jean and her friends. All the shops on the main street had closed by now but the road was still fully parked, which meant I had to drive around for a good few minutes before I could find a space to park. When I finally did so, it was further away from the hall than I had hoped.

Still, the directions I had been given were very clear, and there were no clouds in the night sky. After a week of heavy rain, it was a relief not to have to carry a raincoat and an umbrella. As I approached the small hall, lit by a sharp light over the doorway, I could see Jean and the figure of another woman standing just outside. As the sound of my footsteps warned them of my approach, they both moved out to greet me.

"Hello Roy," said Jean, "I'd like to introduce you to my best friend, Antoaneta."

We shook hands and briefly exchanged pleasantries as we walked towards the door, and into the main body of the hall. It was a large room, with wooden flooring that squeaked as I walked over it. There were more parents than I had expected, and I was happily surprised to see almost as many fathers as there were mothers. I was ushered to meet a rather forbidding looking lady on a stage. I think she would have half terrified me if she did not have deeply kind eyes.

Nevertheless, this lady was obviously in charge, for she soon called attention to the room, and within a moment I found myself alone on the stage facing about a hundred or a hundred and fifty men and women of different ages. Older people, presumably grandparents, were holding smaller children on their knees, while one or two younger parents were obviously trying to keep their children from running around. It looked complete bedlam, and I loved it.

I don't mind children being themselves, and besides, I needed the mothers to keep their thoughts on me, so I explained that it was quite all right to let the children be free. Almost immediately, one boy shot in front of me followed by a laughing younger girl. They were happy, and there is nothing better for me than to see children happy. So, I began.

"Dear Ladies and Gentleman, and friends," I gave a slight look of acknowledgement towards Jean and her friend, who were sitting to the side of the room. Peter was not there, but he was to come later, "Thank you for coming to meet me. I am here to offer thoughts about how your children could do better in school, and to share with you some concerns you may have."

Instantly, a lady on the front row raised her hand, "Would you please excuse me a moment? I think I've left my car lights on." There was a mummer of laughter, as the lady stood up and rushed out of the hall. This was beginning to be like a real classroom, I thought.

And so, to keep the act going and take control of the situation, I immediately pressed the button on the small remote control I had been given. A projector, stationed halfway down the hall, came on and a moment later, the image of a rather developed foetus appeared inside the womb of a mother.

"What is important," I began, "is not to focus on the grades, the performance or the supposed intelligence of a child at any age. To begin to understand the child, we need to understand how they came to be at the moment we are witnessing them. Intelligence," – I turned from the eyes of the audience to the image on the screen – "begins, in one sense by about the 30th week of gestation."

A man on the second row raised his hand, "Excuse me, But how do you know intelligence begins when the baby is still inside the mother? I mean you can't give it a pen, can you?" There was slight laughter in the room, but I smiled too. The atmosphere needed to be kept alive.

It was, however, a good question, and I tried to answer it quickly to keep the attention of the rest of the audience.

"We know that by the 30th week, the foetus is able to remember a sound for ten minutes. By the 34th week, they are able to recall a sound they heard four weeks ago. Since the foetus has an active memory at this time, and since you cannot have intelligence without memory, it seems reasonable to suggest that the intelligence process begins at about the 30th week. But there is a lot more to this that I later need to explain."

As the father seemed content with my explanation, and a little proud, he was able to demonstrate to his wife sitting next to him that he would know what was going on, I continued.

In doing, so I explained how the brain of the yet unborn child begins to take shape through the environmental signals it receives. How defused light entering the embryonic sac begins to organise the visual system. How the sounds about the mother are used by the unborn child to be aware of sensory information, distant bangs, television, and music.

I told them how listening to Mozart was known to improve spatial temporal reasoning skills, the means to be good at logical thinking and so mathematics, and how, when this was played to the foetus, it would organise their neurons in specific ways, and so why they should be aware of the effect to the baby of the kind of music they listen to. Loud rock music I explained is known to cause difficulty in remembering, and this because neurons develop erratic networks. I explained how songbirds actually grow new nerve cells when they sing, and how this alters the size and shape of their brain. What many seemed to find interesting, was how I explained that the way songbirds learn their song is very similar to the way in which we learn the sounds of speech.

Everyone applauded a young boy who, at that moment, suddenly tried to imitate a bird singing, until, that is, his mother told him to be quiet and apologized to me.

"Not a problem," I smiled.

"Speech," I explained, "is a component of language, and this is one of the foundations of intelligence."

Then, and most importantly, I talked to the audience about how the emotions of the mother are picked up by her baby, which is still a part of her, and how the chemicals from these emotions are fed to her foetus to begin to organise the various threshold levels for the neurotransmitters in its brain. This is the chemical means that allow the later child to develop an emotional state and the only means by which a signal can move through the neurons of the brain to process information and give results.

I pressed the button again, and the immortal words of John Fiske appeared on the screen.

"What is the meaning of the fact that man is born into the world, more helpless than any other creature, and more in need of a much longer season than any other living thing, the tender care and wise counsel of its elders?"[10]

"You see," I said as I pointed to the screen, "Fiske tells us that we are not just born and instinctively learn or react, but that, we have to learn how to learn, and the child does this in the first instance from the skills they acquire through their parents."

After a moment, I pressed the button again and another image came upon the screen.

"This," I explained, "is, of course, the newborn child, about a week old."

A gentle murmur of adoration arose from the audience, mostly I thought from the mothers in the room.

"Yes, the newborn is quite adorable. But do you know that this is a genetic strategy that evolved through nature to ensure the survival and not neglect of the newborn?

As you know, all newborns smile, gurgle, have a 'newborn' smell, and cry. All these bond the caregiver to protect the newborn."

"I don't feel that at two o'clock in the morning!" A man's voice shouted from somewhere in the back.

We all laughed.

"But it's true," I answered back, with a smile I could not suppress.

"The infant has four very specific cries," I began again, "One type of cry means they want to be fed. Another cry means they want to sleep. A third, they are frightened and want protection, and a fourth, they want attention. This is the beginning of their skill in language.

Now, depending upon the success of the protection and attention the infant achieves through their strategies of bonding, they will notice the interactive strategies they recognise in the ones they have bonded to. As they become more mobile, they will use these strategies to form an elementary scaffold for their later interaction with the world. This is what we will eventually come to call their 'intelligence'.

There are, then two very important points I would like to explain here:

Firstly, this process, which I call 'imprinting', is the mechanism by which the baby begins to learn to be human. It is also, as I have just said the beginning of a structure by which the human being begins to devise their intelligence with the world in which they live. This is a process that does not stop throughout their life.

Secondly, it is a developmental process that is heavily dependent upon emotion. The quality of love, security, kindness and happiness that they, as human being perceive and experience as they develop, will set the benchmarks for the production levels of the chemicals within their brain that will allow them to process information. We call these chemicals neurotransmitters, and it's these that will most importantly give them the desire to want to interact with their world, and much determines how well they develop to do this.

Throughout thirty years of working with children and studying the development of their ability, the key I have realized is to understand how the psychology of the mind drives the physiology of the body and the brain, in other words, the power of the mind. So, please don't think too much about what the child may or may not have inherited, think far, far more about how you can explain the world to them in a secure and fascinating way.

But just to return to the baby stage for a moment, I would like to show you how vital this interaction is between the mother and her child at the very youngest age. We have found that when infants were neglected by their mother, they were so emotionally lost that they developed their ability to move very slowly. Some infants who had been so neglected were found not to be able to sit-up before they were 21 months of age, while others could not walk before they were three years old."

As I pressed the button, other images of children of different ages came upon the screen. Each looked hollow, as I wanted the audience to really understand the importance of love in development, and, of course, in intelligence.

In bringing the image of a father reading a story to a baby on to the screen, I could move on with my explanation.

"As the baby (and again this is true for any age) feels emotional security, they will be more aware of the world about them. So, if the caregiver or the teacher in school, can direct this sensitivity of awareness to a specific process they wish to explain, which means to teach them something, then the baby, child, or the student will be far better able to learn. Before we go any further, I want to share with you a simple understanding.

The human being does not just give an answer. They do not just give a response or naturally construct what we take to be their effort. Firstly, the child has developed strategies to examine information. They do this mentally through their interest and ability to control distractions, and biologically, which is to say the ways their brain cells and brain chemistry has developed. Now, as you can understand, the more interested they are the more sensitively they will examine something.

As they are sensitive in their mental description of things, so they will bring into the design of their brain more efficient processing systems and a higher architectural structure of memory by which information will be better classified. As they encounter similar information at a later time, they will relate this to their previous experiences and so produce a response. The more sensitive they are in their history of this, the more accurate and faster they will be.

Secondly, children learn how to explain their mind to others, firstly from those who raise them, then from their friends, and finally by how well they feel emotionally secure with their teachers. Through these interactions, they learn how to recognise information, and how to explain their mind to others. This is the very background behind how well they come to present their composition in English, and so how they will be evaluated when they write their reports in geography, physics and history etc.

We can see from this that the ability of the child in school is dependent upon two factors. Emotion, which we have briefly examined, and language; the ways the world in which they live and must survive in are explained to them through the tactics and strategies of those they interact with. This is from the nursing mother right up to the university lecturer."

It was as I said this, that I noticed Jean indicating a little frantically to me that the refreshments were now ready, and so we took a break. But as I stepped down from the stage a number of people, mainly mothers, moved to ask me questions.

Jean came a moment later, and in excusing herself managed to pass me a cup of black coffee and some biscuits from a box. I gratefully accepted and spent the following ten minutes relaxing and talking with members of the audience. As people were beginning to return to their seats, I walked back onto the stage and asked for everyone's attention.

"Before we move on," I announced, "I would like to explain something very clearly. There have been a lot of studies on the intelligence of young children. Most of these were done to try to prove that intelligence is more inherited than it is not. The idea behind this was that the younger the child, the less their intelligence could be said to be developmental and so the more inherited.

But as we have just seen, and as a very simple demonstration, the ability of the human child to adapt begins the moment they are born. Think, then, about the importance of the mother not neglecting her baby, and how variations of attention develop the emotion and psychology of the developing infant to interact with their world. Intelligence is not a thing that just switches on. It develops as the brain develops and the mind explores.

In the 1930s, a psychologist named Nancy Bayley began to study how infants develop. She created the Bayley Test, which is still regarded to be one of the best means to understand a young child's rate of development. For over 50 years, Bayley studied the reactions of thousands of children, in which time she came to realise that it's impossible to predict the intelligence of young children. Below two years of age, infants did not show any stability in the things said to make up intelligence. There is simply no clear pattern to judge their ability by at this age. And, whatever predictions were made upon later children of two, three, four, or five years of age, these were all later found to have changed dramatically.

There is no stability in the ways young children think. That stability in thinking, and so what we call intelligence, only begins once they enter school, because in school the child moves through a very self-limiting and condition-able world, as they spend each day in the same environment and share this with the same children, as they role-play to what is expected of them for their acceptance. If we can understand, or at least begin to, that intelligence is not a fixed thing that belongs to a child, but a thing that is conditioned by the world the human being lives through, then we can begin to understand how parents begin the shaping of their child's intelligence by the quality of love and the complexity of language skills they raise them in.

The problem is because we love our children and do our best for them, that we do not realise how we are a product of the ways we were raised ourselves and how this is a factor of social conditioning. But if we could pull ourselves out from where we are, and look down on how different parents give love to their child and how each raises them with different language skills, then we would really understand how we could learn to do our job better."

A hand shot up from a woman in the third row, "Excuse me!" Many in the room turned to look at her, as she said in an angry tone, "I am sorry to interrupt you, but you make it sound as if we don't love our kids."

I could understand the protectiveness of this mother, and I sympathised with her feelings.

"We all love our children," I responded calmly. "But may I ask you a question?"

The lady nodded, stern-faced.

"Did you shout at your child today?"

Her reply came after a short silence.

"Well, he was playing up a bit."

"So, we too are human. We get tired, stressed and little children can easily get out of control, as they are driven by energy we really wish we had at times. Of course, you shouted, we all do or have done. Although, what we do not realise at that time, is the effect our anger has on the mind of the child. I can clearly remember my mother being very angry with me when I was six, and that was many, many decades ago. Love is not just worrying if our children are safe and protecting them the best we can, it's also how we show that love. I so much wish someone had told me when I was a young father, to try to understand the mind of my child before I got angry with them, not to react with anger because I was tired and stressed with their behaviour, but to try to reason with them."

"How can you reason with a two-year-old in a fit of a temper?" Another woman asked from further back.

"Love. Just give love, patience and kindness."

"It's easy to say," said a man, near the front.

"You know, I was once walking across a field," I said to the audience and to no one in particular, "I had walked many miles and was tired. It was a hot day. Suddenly, I came to a turnstile and on the other side stood a huge bull. There was no way I would cross that turnstile because the bull was right up against it. What could I do? The thought of going all the way back to find another route seemed too much, and yet the thought of going in the field with the bull worried me. I mean, you never know how the bull would react. Sometimes they can be very placid, But well, other times they can be very dangerous. I stood there facing the bull, separated only by a thin metal railing and lines of bared wire. What could I do?

The answer came and I felt a sense of peace come over me. Then, in a very, very calm and low voice, I said 'Hello'. I repeated this one word many, many times, each time with the same calmness, sense of peace and genuine love. I don't know how long it took. It seemed like a very long time standing there, but suddenly and slowly the bull stretched its head closer to me.

Very carefully, and I was nervous, I reached across the fence and gently stroked its head. All the time I repeated this one word 'Hello'. I don't know why I chose this word. It was just the one that came into my head. But I know now, that it was the gentle way that I said the word that won the heart of the bull, because the bull moved its huge body to the side so that I could open the gate of the turnstile and feel I could walk into the field. I was actually really, really nervous, but I told myself to keep calm and just give love."

A strange silence had come over the entire room. People were just staring at me. Then, a lady in the front row took charge and changed the direction of the atmosphere.

"Can you please tell me what you mean by language skills? I don't really understand."

"Language," I replied, "in the sense of intelligence, is not English or French. It's the words, feelings and gestures by which we share our mind with another. In one sense, it's grammatical, the quality and variety of words used and so how well the meaning of a sentence is defined and conveyed. In another, it's cultural by the expressions that have evolved through the work and life of a group of people."

"So, what do we do?" a man asked from somewhere at the back of the room.

"Read stories. In the simplest and most direct way read, tell, but more importantly, create stories with your child. Give them a life of adventure, inspire them, and the tools, the words, to make their own exploration. The greater variety of words you share with your child the more they will learn, and the better they will be to make sense of our world.

Storytelling is so important," – I really emphasised this when I spoke – "and a child should be told a story overnight. I didn't stop with my children until they were in their early teens. Stories build up vocabulary, new and different words and they develop experience in relating to different scenarios. This is important in enabling the later child in school to be faster to associate to information they are given but also in enabling them to present their mind in different ways as they answer questions.

In fact, it is really how well the student has composed their essay, told their story, that they are much evaluated upon and so marked. This skill we have with words," I added, "tends to be one we were raised in by our parents and this was decided by the level of their education and the job they did, just as the skill we impart to our children comes from the kind of education we had and the job we do."

"What has the job to do with it?" asked a man who looked to be the grandfather of a small girl he was holding on his knee.

"The job that we do takes over the ways we think about the world and how we should react to people in it. If you are an accountant, salesman, police officer, or plumber, you will tend to use the language of your world when you come home and give shape to the language you are developing your child in.

This," I added, "has got nothing to do with social status, as a job tends to imply. I am talking here about the sensitivity in defining and describing information. An accountant, for instance, has to be very precise with information and they will raise their child to think about what they are about to do and to constantly check what they have done, raising them on the awareness of errors. A salesman will have developed a play with words and emotions to add colour to a story. A police officer will use very understandable and plain words, and so teach exactness in helping another to understand their mind very clearly. A plumber, for example, will be vaguer in their use of words and with the range of vocabulary they use, because their job requires them to work more alone and with easier descriptions."

"What about a teacher?" Someone shouted from the back. We all laughed at that, myself included.

"But all this is in a general sense," I continued seriously, "The plumber, for instance, may read extensively and love crosswords. They may guide their children to understand how things come apart, can be put back together again and so work. They can inspire their child to a fascination with the world about them, while the accountant can be so busy they have too little time for their child and suddenly become horrified in how their child has become addicted to video games, lost interest in their studies, and closed themselves within a human less world."

"That is a real problem!" said a lady to my right.

"Indeed it is," I agreed, "I meet an increasing number of parents who do not know how to control the time their children spend on these 'devil boxes'. What began as innocent fun, very quickly took over their sense of reality and by the addiction they create, children lose sensitivity in their emotions with others. They become more self-centred because they have less feedback to cause them to be more caring and thoughtful. Very seriously, this addiction pulls them away from thinking about and wanting to keep up with their schoolwork."

I could see that many people in the audience were very interested in this, so I expanded upon what I was saying.

"You see," I explained, "when our child is born; we devote our lives to them. We race home from work to enjoy each moment we can with them. Our pleasure in life is to watch them explore, laugh with joy and study their fascination with a story. As the child grows and moves through school, we hardly notice the detachment whereby they spend more time with their friends than with us.

Such is as life must be, and so we focus on our job and work hard. As work overtakes our mind, we find other ways to make our child happy than with our presence. So, we buy them things whereby they can amuse themselves, one of which today must be a game console. Their excitement pleases us, for we know we have made them happy. They play and we work, but our balance with work and our time with them becomes distorted.

Too many parents I have met ask me to help them with this problem because they do not know how to regain the time and the love they once had with their child. As the world of each has become disentangled, the parent's worry turns to anguish in realisation, they no longer can reach the mind and heart of their child, because their child has now become absorbed, addicted, into a world that is not real. The excitement of the game compels them to play, not to lose with fun, but to win, always to win, and then to the next level.

The means to break the spell that has caught our child, and is responsible for their too little interest in school, and so, their falling grades, eludes us. If we try to rationalise with our child to spend less time with their game, we fail because the possession held over them. They can go into moods we do not understand or erupt in an outburst that frightens us. What do we do? The answer came very clearly to me one day,"

I said as I looked at the interesting faces before me, "A teacher who has devoted her life to teaching children lost her time with her own child. In fact, she became a principal at a very large school, and one day this very stressed and exhausted mother brought her son to meet me. I remember very clearly meeting the boy, who was about 15 at the time, and asking him what he likes to do."

"Um, I don't know," He told me.

Now, I knew that he liked to play computer games. In fact, this is really all he did.

"Do you like fishing?" I asked him. A spark of interest came into his eyes, and so the three of us considered how the mother could spend time with her son making models, playing a sport or going fishing. Now, the next morning, this busy principal called me and said that this idea had made her very stressed.

"I don't have time for fishing," she told me.

"What you are telling me," I said, "is that you don't have time for your son. Now, you think only of work. Work has taken over your life, and because of this, you have lost the one thing that really matters to you, your son."

"But I don't know anything about fishing," she pleaded.

What I could really understand here is that the parent had lost the sense of adventure she used to have with her son. Overworked, tired, exhausted with meetings and dealing with people problems, she had lost the sense of adventure that creates meaning in a relationship.

"So, learn," I told her, "It's the learning together, the sharing of doing something vital to rebuild your relationship. Your son asks you, 'Mum, (or Dad) how do you do this?' And, you ask your son, 'How shall we do this?' This sharing of a problem is the knitting together of a relationship. It's the very small day to day things that bond, not the magical trip to Disneyland once in a blue moon. So, you ask how to tie a knot in the fishing line, and together you try. Maybe the knot does not hold, and you both need to keep trying, or get help. But it is the act of sharing that creates the memory. What better way to learn to understand each other," I added, "can there be than to sit and watch afloat for hours on end; things to talk about, problems released, ideas developed, purposes germinated, and things to plan."

"Great," she told me, and then said, "I'll go and get a fishing rod next week."

"Next week?" I queried. "It's Friday night now. You could get the rod and tackle tomorrow morning with your son, and by Saturday afternoon, you could be living the adventure that will bond you together again."

"But the weather forecast tomorrow says rain," she told me.

I remember how I smiled to myself at that time because I said to her, "It's often when things go wrong that you remember the funny, happy incidents that bond, and which bring the pleasure of a relationship many, many years later."

The looks about me were very contemplative. I could imagine too many of the parents searching their soul here. It is just so simple to fall into this trap.

"Well, how did 'you' deal with it?" It was the same woman as before who asked me the question.

"It was very hard," I had to agree, "My children played very happily together. I bought them a computer screen and a games console, thinking it would help them to learn. The first game I bought was about finding things and developing an understanding of search patterns. Within a few weeks, they had found more exciting games to play.

I was working upstairs when suddenly I thought World War Three had started in the room where they played the computer. I raced down and disconnected the cables. The girls went to do other things, but feeling that I was punishing them too much I reconnected the cables the next day. However, it was not long after this before the war really did begin. Hearing a sharp scream and fighting, I raced down again. I knew then that I could not limit them on their time with these games, because they would find excuses to progressively gain more and more time. I had to get this game thing out of our lives!

So, I took the screen, game console and threw them in a pond in the garden. I just knew that if I did not completely destroy the equipment that one way or another it would be back again. Well, I thought that my drastic action would have caused my girls to have a meltdown, but by the time I had walked back into the house, each was happily doing things in their own room. After that computer went out of our lives, peace came in."

"And, what do your daughters do now?" asked the lady again.

"One," I laughed. "Is a computer expert!"

The hall burst into laughter.

"Did they ever forgive you?" a man asked.

"Well, she makes my website now, and she helps me with all computer things I have no clue about," I said with a smile.

"But to be serious here," – I wanted to bring things back on track – "there really is a big difference in the vocabulary higher-income parents tend to raise their children in, compared with those who don't earn so much money.

What this means is that once the children of the better-off parents enter school, they are already further advanced in language skills than those of other parents. This enables them to adapt faster to information, settle in easier to the requirements of the school mind, and so do better in their schoolwork. As the year goes by year this difference seldom changes, which is one of the reasons why children from better homes are more likely to go to university. They are not born more intelligent, but they are often created so by the better environments they live through."

"Does this mean that if I don't have a lot of money, my girl won't go to university?" asked a concerned looking young lady before me.

"No, Not at all," I reassured her. "Statistics are one thing. They just tell the general story, but it is you who decides what will happen. More often, the father will be working more hours away from home, and so it's the mother who is more likely to have more time with their child.

We know that it is the mother who will inspire, counsel and guide the child to success, inspire them with a purpose for doing the small things that encourage larger things to occur, to praise them when things go wrong and so encourage them to understand the importance of not giving up. To instil in them a sense of discipline for the things that need to be done, and done the best way they can be. To make the time to help them to understand the developing world that surrounds them. To listen to their worries, fears, and help them to overcome their insecurities. To be careful of the friends they make, and the dangers of the world their friends can pull them into, by which I mean here computer gaming and smoking, but we must also today consider the danger of experimenting with drugs.

And, most of all, when the child is young and badly behaved, to listen carefully to their heart and to explain by reason what should be done, instead of shouting at them and not realising how we could disturb their mind.

Yesterday, I saw a young mother pushing her pram with a girl of about three years old following behind. The child could not keep up, and the mother was in a bad temper shouting at the child in the street. There was no understanding of heart here, only the adult angry and frustrated and the child being mentally abused for being a child. Love is the most important thing a mother can raise her child on; not just by saying I love you, but also by touching with tender care. The child will need this in the world they will soon come to face."

"I want to understand this clearly," said a woman at the far back of the room, "Does this mean the mother is solely responsible for the child's intelligence in school?"

"You know," I replied, "I once read a book called 'The Prophet'. It was written by a man called Kahlil Gibran, and it told the simple story of people asking a wise man about life. There was one part I remember where the wise man was asked to explain about children. I don't recall the exact wording, but Gibran explained that it was the parent who put the arrow to the bow and fired it. But once the arrow had left the bow, it would find its own way to the target. I think what Gibran was trying to show here was that the parent can help the child to understand the world, but it's the world the child moves through that will shape them. The phrase 'you launch your children as living arrows' comes to mind."

"Could you give me an example?" This time it was Jean's friend who asked the question.

"Well, the obvious one is bullying. The one that is not is divorce."

There was a feeling of understanding within the people in front of me. A few nodded their heads. All listened.

"Let's think about divorce first. All partners argue. They may love each other intently, but they each have their own needs. When the needs of one restrict the needs and hopes of another there is conflict, unless there is a measure of freedom and joint respect. When parents argue with each other, the child's mind is thrown into insecurity. They are frightened of what will happen to the world they know. It is important for this reason that if you fight with each other, that you manage to escape to a room where your child is less likely to hear you.

Please do not fight or shout at each other in front of your child. You will do more damage than you can imagine, for those disturbing impressions may stay in your child's mind for the rest of their life. The tragedy for the child is when the parents decide they can no longer live together, and they start to fight over who the child belongs to. This rips the heart of the child. If I may suggest anything here, it is not to fight for ownership, but to let the child be free to join the parent they want to when they want to. Try to give them freedom through love.

I once met a brother and sister in their mid-thirties. They explained to me that when they were children their parents divorced and how this had destroyed the beautiful happy world they had known. Over the years that followed, they lost purpose in their lives and each struggled to know who they are. The girl felt she wanted to help other children who had the pain she had, and this drove her to study very hard. She became very successful academically, and eventually became a social worker.

Her brother did not have this purpose and drifted with great insecurity through his childhood and teens. He found no interest in anything and certainly not in his schoolwork. When he left school, his passes were so low he could not get a job easily. Eventually, he got a job as a shop assistant stacking shelves. The world of this brother and sister is now financially totally different, and each are opening different avenues of opportunity for the children they have. But every night, each still goes to bed with a pain in their heart. Now, I would like to explain to you what really happened in their brains through this stress, and so what happens to the brain of a bully's victim."

I paused for a moment, to take a drink of water from the glass that had been placed on the table beside me by Jean.

"For most children in school," – I could feel or perhaps hear that my voice was sorrowful now – "bullying is a concern that is not really understood. When we think of a child being bullied, we think of the fear they have of being hurt or socially embarrassed. Too few of us realise the process that occurs within their brain. In a simple sense, but also as an extremely important way to understand how intelligence works, we can say that the mind seeks security for the protection of the body, and also for the protection of the identity of the personality.

When the child receives love their mind is secure, and the chemicals of their brain operate as they have developed to do through their life experiences to date. But, should the child receive a threat, this can be from a bully to injure them or by a snide remark that hurts their feelings and so social acceptance, and their mind can trigger off changes in the chemistry of their brain." I pressed the button, and the following image came upon the screen.

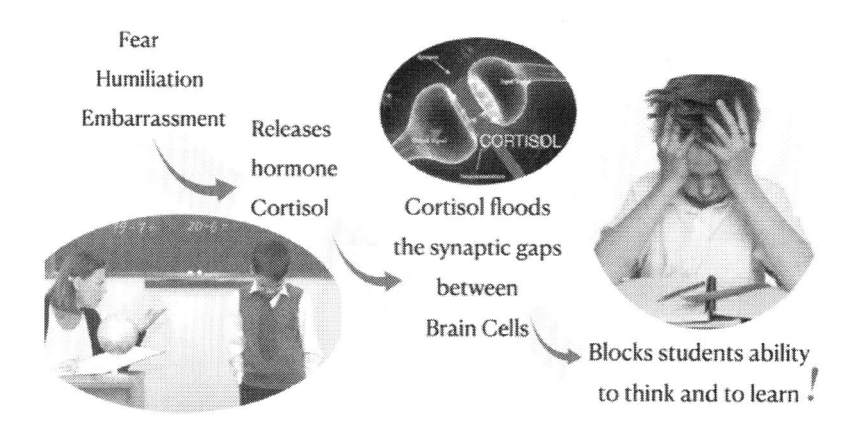

Fear
Humiliation
Embarrassment   Releases hormone Cortisol

Cortisol floods the synaptic gaps between Brain Cells

Blocks students ability to think and to learn !

I explained to the people in front of me how cortisol works (as we discussed earlier in this book).

Many were very interested to see a visual image of the real effect of bullying. It was, as a lady later told me, only through this that she could really understand what it meant to be bullied.

The attention of the audience was disrupted by the loud voice of a man who had only recently entered the hall.

"What has this got to do with intelligence?" he asked as he took a seat next to a woman with two children.

"Let me explain it this way," I replied, "there was a case of a psychologist who examined two identical twins. Now, because of the belief that intelligence is inherited, it's reasoned that identical twins will have the same kind of intelligence, after all, they can come from the same genetic egg. However, with these twins, one was very clearly more intelligent than the other.

It was discovered that the one who displayed less ability and gained far lower grades than their brother had a long history of being bullied. Examination showed a disturbing level of cortisol in his brain. As we have seen, once cortisol rises, it disturbs the child's ability to concentrate on the movement of information. Basically, this is because their mind is thinking too much about the danger of the bully. So, this twin was less able than their brother to concentrate on information or process it very well.

Equally, this lower performance made them less secure and so less proficient when they presented their thoughts. And, really, it is how well a student presents their thoughts when they take an examination or give any kind of response that their ability is judged upon. Intelligence is not what is thought of it," – I paused for a moment, to let this sink in, before saying –

"It's a feature that can change if the personality desires it so and has the opportunity for this, but this is not apparent because we seldom change environments. As the child will live through the same environment at home, so will they in school. They will go to the same classes day after day and hold the same social recognition with those in their class and with their teachers. Their environment very seldom changes, but change the environment, and you can change the intelligence, one way or the other."

I cast a look at the father, but he gave no indication he had seen the significance in what I had said. So, I expanded a little further.

"In a very broad sense, we can see from this example of a child being bullied how any child's ability to recognise and process information is rooted in their emotional stability, in other words, the chemicals in their brain. Their ability to present their understanding to another lies in the language skills they have built up through their emotional content. It's not quite as simple as this in reality, because emotion and language overlap, but in a general sense it is like this.

Now, how well the student can explain their mind to their teachers when they talk to them or when they write something, which is to say their ability with language, is the only means by which the teacher or the system will judge their worth. Thus, the assessments that arise from class marks and examinations are used, however, loosely we might like to think, to suggest how intelligent a child is and so what kind of job they could do. Never lose track of what school is about," – I stressed the point.

"It's not really about how to help all children to learn better so they can have a happier life. It is really about who can do what kind of job, once they leave school. So, the child who gets 9/10 repeatedly will be thought of as more intelligent than the one who never gets higher than 6/10, but the root cause of these different grades is not intelligence but skills in language and these skills are based on the level of emotional harmony each student had while they learned each part of the skill of language."

I cast a look at Jean and noticed she was pointing to her watch. Time had gone faster than I realized, so I briefly informed those in the audience of the real responsibility they have in the emotional and language development of their children, and so not to think to leave it up to the teacher who has 30 children in 45 minutes to try to explain everything to. I wound up the evening by asking, "Does anyone have a question?"

A series of hands shot up.

"You said stories are important. Please tell me again why?" the question came from a serious-looking young man on my left.

"Well, when a child listens to a story," I responded, "they are not just happy. Stories will develop their skills in sharing thoughts. They give them experiences to understand better how to relate to the mind of others. Stories develop oral skills, increase vocabulary, improve word recognition, and teach them how to plan a series of events, as well as how to interpret those of another."

I noticed then that he was writing this down. So, I gave clear points to the audience at large.

"Stories increase the number of words a child knows.

They raise their familiarity with words.

Stories cause children to recognise how words link, and so give words higher levels of association.

They also improve a child's ability to more readily grasp a meaning given to them.

As the child's mind becomes absorbed in a story, they realise how to put a series of events in order. This teaches them how to present their thoughts to another. We must remember here that the child does not just think. They develop to learn how to do this.

I remember a study by UNICEF, which showed that children who had learned to read better at the age of seven than other children, did better in intelligence tests later in adolescence.

But again, it's not just reading that is important. What is also important is that they share the thoughts they have gained from what they have read with their parents or friends, and so can expand upon the understanding they have gained. Explaining your mind to others helps you to better understand what you mean.

So, stories improve the child's awareness that different people want to hear their mind in different ways.

In other words, stories teach them how to better formulate their thoughts. So, they improve the child's level of articulation, and, of course, their means of expression, which is what, school is looking for.

But beyond all these, stories inspire their imagination. This is vital to the child because imagination inspires the confidence to want to explore. In turn, this creates the courage for the child to take risks, and thereby develop through mistakes learned."

A lady to my right asked, "You have just mentioned intelligence tests, but I thought you said intelligence can't be measured?"

"I was merely following the general belief here to express the point. Personally, I would have preferred to say tests of mental competence, after all we can compare and measure the performance of a child at any age. But the idea of an intelligence test is that ability is more or less constant throughout life. This means that if you measure the performance of an older child, that the score you make of them will be the same when they are thirty or fifty. This is wrong. Intelligence changes as the world of the mind changes."

"What do you mean their world changes?" This time the question came from an elderly lady in the middle of the audience.

"In one sense, it could be to change the child's school. In another, it could be just to change their teacher. In another, it could be for a divorced mother and father to remarry. We must forget the idea of regarding the child's ability in school as something they were born with. And, hold on to the reality of the child's mind struggling to feel safe and happy amongst the minds of others, who try to share their thoughts with them through the skills they have developed. This is as true for the parents of the child as it is to their teachers in school."

"What do you mean teacher in school?" The question was asked with a suspicious voice, from a rather senior looking gentleman.

"A teacher is a human being. Any teacher is no different than a hairdresser or artist when it comes to their skill. Some will have learned their job through the rules they were trained in, while others will know how to intuitively learn to do this job, they will listen to their heart. It is the sensitivity of the teacher in knowing how to reach the sensitivity of the minds of their students, that gives them quality in how they teach, not just being a teacher. We are all human and we all need to learn. I meet many teachers who do not know or have long forgotten how to reach the heart of their students. Others have lost interest in their job. We can see this in the high percentage of teachers who leave education. Teaching is no longer what many expect it to be."

"Does it matter what kind of food I give to my son to make him clever?" The question came from a young mother, holding a small boy on her knee, and so brought a new direction to the thinking in the hall.

I looked at the mother and the way she held her son. It was easy to see her concern.

"Well, the body and so the brain is just a machine, it will work on the fuel it's given. So, in one sense a well-balanced diet will help the brain to operate more efficiently, and in this sense, yes, the type of food you give is important. But this alone will not make him clever. What really is important is the psychology upon which he is raised. Emotion drives everything. Your child may be raised on a poor nutritional diet, but if you raise him with love, tenderness and security, and you take the time to help him with great sensitivity to understand what others mean and the ways of the world, this will be a million times more important in the development of his intelligence."

"I read somewhere that coffee raises IQ," said the young man who a moment earlier had asked about stories.

"It's very important to understand why that statement is wrong, even though it was made very recently by a prominent psychologist. I remember reading that too. You see, first of all, IQ is not intelligence."

Because of the previous few questions about intelligence, I needed to explain to this man and so the people in the hall, just as I had earlier to Jean, that IQ is only an abbreviation for the Intelligence Quotient Test.

"This Intelligence Quotient Test," I further stated, "is only a theoretical way to calculate intelligence. There are many people who do not agree with what is measured in this test, and even that intelligence can be measured.

You know, if you read a psychology book today, it will most likely say that a French psychologist in the early 20th Century, by the name of Alfred Binét, designed the very first intelligence test. This is not correct. Binét only designed a way of estimating if a child who was performing poorly in school was doing so because of their developmental background or if they may have some neurological condition that was holding back their ability. In fact, this is what the whole idea of IQ does. The word IQ causes us to see intelligence as limited, and so we move through a mindset that creates environments that shackle a child's understandings to the past they developed through.

We must know then, that while Binét is too often said to be the father of intelligence testing, that he never actually made a test for intelligence. For Binét understood that intelligence is not stable enough to be measured. In fact, because he realized how malleable it is, he insisted that children should be taught how to develop their skills in learning from the moment they begin school. Our belief that intelligence is stable enough to be measured came about through psychologists, mainly in America, who were using this belief to drive political policies, as some still do today.

I mention this, because once we move away from the rigid idea of IQ and move to see intelligence as highly modifiable, and I really mean that it is, and then we can understand better how it develops.

So, to come back to your question, coffee does not change the IQ, but it can temporarily raise the performance level of intelligence. You see, caffeine is a stimulant that helps the mind to concentrate. By concentrating more, a person can understand better. It's very simple. But once they stop drinking coffee, their concentration will go down as their thoughts will more drift to take interest in the movement of life. So, yes, Caffeine can improve intelligence, but not the way you have been raised to understand this meaning."

Jean was moving towards the door and beginning to wave a little frantically to me to wind up the evening. She had told me in the break that she had promised to have the hall locked up by 9:30. So I stepped down from the small stage, but as I did so two women stood up and moved towards me.

The first lady was a little older than the other and wore a bright red coat that lit up the greyness in the old village hall. She was blond and had hair over her shoulders. She was small and petit, but her hand was very strong when she put it into mine.

"I find your talk on intelligence very interesting," she told me, "I had never thought of it in this way before. I just thought of intelligence as something we have, and I suppose most of it coming from our parents."

"This is a general idea that most people have. In fact, it is one that has been carefully cultivated within our societies, as I tried to hint at here."

She leaned her head to one side, looked slightly puzzled, "What do you mean cultivated?"

I had put myself into a trap, I realized. It was so easy to say something, but then to explain why could take the time I did not then have.

"Well, societies are very political," I said, giving Jean a wave to tell her I was coming. "As people look after themselves, and the group they feel that best serves their interest. The higher roles and rewards in society used to be guaranteed by the right of access, money and contacts, but as our technology developed it enabled people from poorer levels to rise through the ranks. The idea that ability and so intelligence is inherited brought some sense of stability to the social situation and the political pressures that were brewing in the 19th Century."

"That's why the Japanese used to behead sailors." I looked down to discover a boy of about ten years old, who had suddenly appeared from behind the red coat of the lady.

The mother looked down at her son and told him to be quiet.

"Well, actually he is correct," I said smiling at the boy's keenness, "The Tokugawa Dynasty in Japan kept the country isolated in order to prevent people, particularly sailors," – I looked down at the boy with a wink – "from bringing in new technology for hundreds of years. They understood how control of technology kept control of social opportunities and so social stability."

"They were quick to learn though," It was the other woman who now joined the conversation.

I nodded politely, and while I knew the Japanese success with technology came from the inspiration of an American in the 1950s, E.W.Deming, I kept my counsel. Jean was now beginning to look more stressed at the doorway. I had to wind up the evening, but could not resist adding that the top educational psychologist in England, a man named Cyril Burt, deliberately falsified test results to try to prove that intelligence was inherited. Based on the false reports he produced, money for schools was diverted to children in richer areas on the basis that those in the poorer areas did not inherit enough intelligence to warrant money being wasted on their educational opportunity.

"Is he still alive?" asked the woman in the red coat.

"No, Not now, but he did influence educational policies for some 75 years in the 20th Century."

"Which country again?" it was the other woman who asked.

"Well, officially he controlled education in England, but in the time in which he lived, this really meant the British Empire from Canada to India to Australia. We can say that most of the world in the 20th century based its belief on children having their intelligence inherited, and money directed away from schools of poorer children to those serving better areas on fabricated lies by Burt and his ilk. There really is quite a history behind this."

"Have you written about this?" asked the woman with the boy again. I took out a copy of 'The Hidden Secrets of Intelligence' from my case and passed it to her with a smile. "Please, with my compliments."

I began to walk towards the doorway and now a quite distressed looking Jean. The two ladies moved by my side. The boy had somehow disappeared.

"But," continued the lady with the red coat, "I really wanted to invite you to meet my friends, we have a group of parents and teachers, I am sure they would love to hear what you say. We need to understand what you say about intelligence affecting the grades our children get."

"Of course," I said, "Please call me tomorrow, and we can make a date." I passed her a card with my contact details and turned to the other lady.

"I am awfully sorry to have kept you."

"Oh, that's quite all right," she said, "I was just wondered if you could come and meet a boy in my class. You see, I don't think he has a brain."

Chapter Eight
Paul

On the way back home, I kept thinking about the words the teacher had used, "He doesn't have a brain." Of course, it was not to mean the boy literally did not have a brain, merely which he appeared not to know how to use it. And yet, I remembered a case I had studied many years earlier, where a young man suffering from hydrocephalus was discovered to have lost some 95% of his brain, and yet was performing very naturally in university.

As I recalled, some of the ventricles in his brain had ceased to conduct properly, and this had caused a build-up of cerebrospinal fluid within his skull. The pressure from this fluid had compressed most of his brain matter to the inner side of his skull, enabling only some five percent to appear to remain intact.

Yet, and despite this extensive damage, he had achieved 126 on an IQ score, just acquired an honours degree in mathematics, and to all other intents and purposes appeared to function very normally. I had written about this case in "Brain Plasticity: How the Brain Learns through the Mind to create Intelligence". As it turned out, the child did have a brain. Paul was eleven years old when I met him for the first time and he seemed, in the words of his teacher, completely stupid.

One thing, I realized immediately was that this boy had a very poor sense of relating to information.

Now, to connect or make some sense of information, we must first know of the world about us and store in our memory parts that we have taken some interest in. This storing relies upon strategies by which information is grouped. So, to think of a shoe, for instance, is to link it with the foot, then leg and so the body, but also with leather, then animal, and also with colour such as brown, black etc. Then, of course, there are different kinds of shoes and different ways a shoe can be made secure on the foot. All this information is built up through an ever-expanding network of information, and yet it is all and in total reliant upon sensitivity in awareness.

As I worked with Paul, I realized that he lived in a world that was so happy for him, that he simply did not make a mental connection with very much in his life. I have, I am deeply grateful to say, never tried a drug of any kind, although I could imagine that under such influence mental impressions of things could have a certain lucidity that prevents clear recognition. In this condition, information would be stored with a disconnected sense, which would make a later association to it vague and of poor quality.

As I watched Paul respond to the different ways I sought to encourage him, it seemed that he was so happy euphorically that he did not connect with the world that was judging him. The question was, why?

In the book I have just mentioned, I reason that intelligence is built up through bonding processes. In fact, one subtitle I thought to use was *In Search of New Understanding for Intelligence*. This bonding process I call imprinting, and I explain how the human being inherits the code for this without any variation of genetic quality. As the child develops in age, so they move through higher levels of complex strategies with this process, to achieve the level of bonding they require with other human beings. As one will find a similarity with the personality of another, so two human beings will create a bond whereby they influence each other in behavioural and intellectual strategies.

As I came to understand the family of Paul, so I realized that his parents were very normal in the sense that they did not think to teach him any skills of development. The father was a happy and contented man, and the mother easily entertained by game shows and soap operas. They were no different than the normal family of today. However, there was one very noticeable difference and this lay with Paul's elder brother.

This brother had suffered oxygen starvation at birth and was slightly retarded because of this. He was very able to do an unskilled job and drive a car, but he, like his parents was a very happy and unstressed young man. This family happiness lay in the ways they accepted the world and lived smoothly within it. They were all really very, very nice people.

As I realized Paul had been left in the care of his brother from a very early age, and as I understand the imprinting process, so I understood that Paul devised his way of analysing the world first through the interactive skills of his slightly retarded brother and then through those of his parents.

With the sense of ease by which he developed, Paul was never stressed to understand his world in a way that would have caused him to build up the more precise memory systems that other children do normally. In consequence of this, he was thought too simple by his teachers, and as other children struggled to respond to the pressures to learn, Paul simply drifted further into his own world. When I met him, he sat in a math's class with a textbook that was one year behind that used by the rest of the class and was totally unsure of how to proceed in the pages given to him by his teacher. In short, Paul needed to learn how to think.

I began to help him in this, by teaching his parents how to be involved in Paul's interaction with the world about him. Naturally enough, I explained to his parents the importance of storytelling. I was astonished to discover that no one in Paul's family had ever read or told him a story.

They simply watched the television, often leaving Paul as a child to fall asleep in front of it. So, with guidelines I created for them, his parents began a process of educating his mind to know how to better recognise events, store them with greater precision in his memory banks, and relate to them to predict future meanings. Within a few months, Paul became an active member of his class, with a new ability to understand the world that was being forced upon him.

Paul's case is discussed in "Intelligence: The Great Lie", and I do not wish to repeat it here, save to say that we found a way to teach this child how to be more aware of the world in which he lives. Within a few weeks, his parents and I, working together, were able to create a great transformation in his ability to learn, and so with the performance, he made in his class, his teacher did discover that Paul did have a brain after all!

Chapter Nine
How to Help Students Get Better Grades

I soon discovered that the name of the lady with the red coat was Laura, and that of her son was called Charlie. In the times I met them, Charlie quite grew on me. He had an inspiring mind, which loved history. This is a passion of mine, or at least it became one once I discovered the social drives behind the names and battles I was boringly told to memorise when I was a child at school.

As I drove into the now almost deserted car park of the large school I had been asked to come to, I saw Laura and Charlie waiting for me. As I greeted Laura, I secretly passed a bar of chocolate to Charlie with a wink and a whisper, "To keep you going."

We walked up three flights of stairs, which made me realise the staff must be very fit to run up and down these so many times a day. Heaving a little and desperately trying not to show it, I followed Laura into a science lab that held a great number of adults placed behind rows of tables, almost the width of the room. It was interesting for me to see Bunsen burners still connected to gas taps with those red rubber hoses, not least because I remembered my physics teacher once whipping me with one of these. But that was in days-gone-by.

The seating of the adults here was, however, not one that I liked. I had hoped to be in a classroom where I could organise the chairs in such a fashion that I could walk freely amongst those who had come. This is a practice I use whenever I teach. However, time was limited, people were sitting expectantly and I had a raised platform in the front, so most could see me if not all hear too clearly. I would have to watch this, I told myself.

First, however, Laura walked me along the length of each table, introducing me to parents, teachers and even the vice principal, which to my pleasant surprise had seated himself right at the back of the room to better watch all that went on.

A lady knocked at the door and beckoned Charlie to join her. I later discovered she was his auntie who would do a jigsaw puzzle with him while they prepared the later refreshments.

After introducing myself to all who had kindly joined me, I walked to the blackboard at the end of the room and once again explained a little of what I had been doing for the past 30 years with children.

I followed this with a short introduction as to why we think intelligence can be known to be inherited in each child, and how intelligence is really a matter of the emotional world of the child through the language skills they acquire. It was from this that I moved to explain the difficulty for the child in the class to learn.

"School grades," I began, "are not really a matter of intelligence. They are more about knowing the rules by which the world of school works, and so how its information can be configured, new meanings have to be related to earlier understandings, formulas learned, items memorised and associations realized. It's for this reason that it's very important that each child keeps up with each lesson as it unfolds. This is, of course, not so easy for the child.

Children, especially the younger, are not robots that we can just feed them with information, although, this is what in essence we do. They have an energy we often desire, and too often struggle against as we try to keep their mind focused on something we are teaching them.

As they become older, their energy will have calmed down, but their mind is none the less easy to control if they lose interest. If and when they do, their mind will drift to other things. Some of these will be good for them, such as the movie they watched last night, who they will play with after school, and as they mature, the boy or girl they hope to date. Of course, bad thoughts will also come, especially if others are saying hurtful things about them or they worry about being bullied.

Yet, this focus is very important for the academic skills they are building up. The more focused they are, the better they will take note and the more likely remember what we are trying to teach them." I turned to the board behind me, and in picking up a white stick of chalk quickly drew this illustration.

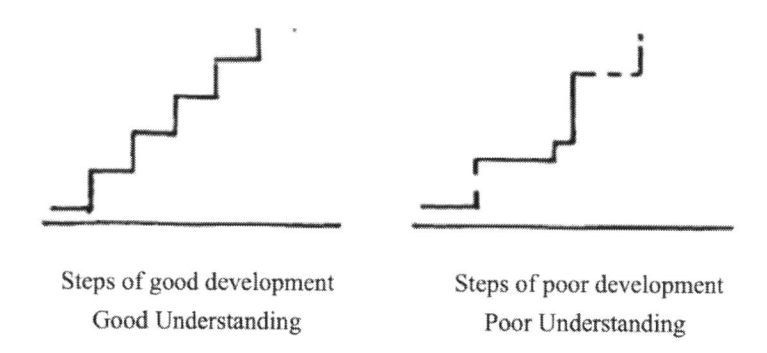

Steps of good development　　Steps of poor development
Good Understanding　　　　　Poor Understanding

"These steps of development," I explained, "do not begin when the child begins a new subject. They can begin when they first learn to organise their mind about how school works, and their understanding of what it expects from them in primary school. This, in turn, can go back to how their parents prepared them for school.

Children, after all, are neither brilliant nor stupid. They are just children trying to understand a world through their values, while we judge them through ours. When we think of either one or the other as a deciding factor in a child's development, we ignore their life history, and so of the world, they had lived through before we come to make judgement upon them.

The world of one will have been good and secure so that as lesson followed lesson all was well understood, checked, and practised at home, their mind lived with this information. The world of another will not have been like this, parts of lessons will have been missed or misunderstood, to leave a mind with little interest in the information of school and one that seeks distraction in freer thoughts.

Now providing the mind of, well, let's say a student, rather than a child here can resist the distractions of hurtful minds and problems at home, they need to follow the information given by their teacher. What happens in reality, is that the student translates the way the teacher conveys their thoughts to the way they have developed to understand information. It is not, as we may think, that one person hears the words of another and understands them or does not. If they do not understand, it's because they are not readily familiar with these words, when they are not they have to try to alter the meaning communicated to them according to the familiarity they have.

I'll give you a simple example. I grew up understanding the meaning of the word 'average', as in an average group of people. However, some people use the word 'mean' instead of 'average', and so would say 'the mean of a group of people'. Now, my mind does not feel happy with the word mean in this sense, so it automatically changes 'mean' to 'average' whenever I come across it, and it is only then that I can relate to what is meant here.

This wordplay of language was once used to purposely complicate the learning process to create different opportunities for children from different social or cultural backgrounds. So, we found that textbooks used a higher level of language which suited children and students who were raised by academically minded parents but hindered the ability of children to understand their lessons that came from working-class homes. There was a great movement, in about the 1980s, to produce textbooks with a common language and with more colourful illustrations so that a wider range of children could understand them easier.

However, as the mind of the student follows the information given by their teacher, they will move through particular phases. Sometimes, they will not hear a word or miss a meaning. Sometimes, their mind will drift on to other things, and sometimes they will not be ready to understand a parcel of information.

It is because of the latter, that it's really vital that parents help their child to keep up with their lessons by going over what they have done in a day. It is also (I looked reassuringly to the teachers

I had been introduced to) really helpful to incorporate some sense of earlier lessons into each current one, to keep the mind of the students aware of the development of the lesson. After all, students will come into your lessons not with minds trying to remember what was covered in previous lessons, but with minds blank and just waiting for you to switch them on."

I took hold of the chalk duster and wiped out the drawing I had just made. A cloud of dust blew out from the board on account of the duster not being cleaned, but it felt good. I have always felt that when my hands are covered with chalk that I have been a teacher. Felt pens on a whiteboard don't give me the same feeling. Anyway, wiping my hands together to clear the dust, I picked up the chalk again and made the following drawing.

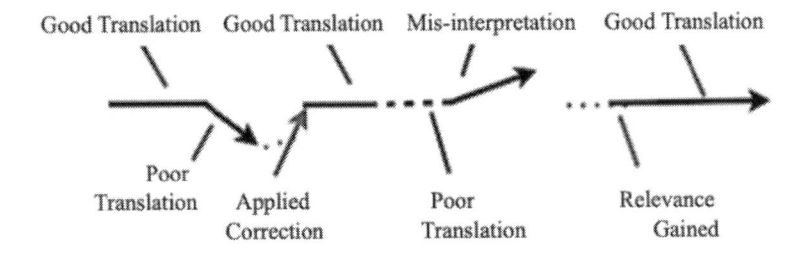

"As you can see here," – I said looking back at the board – "the mind of the student holds a good translation between how the teacher explains their mind and how the student is able to lock into their thoughts. But then something goes wrong, and a poor translation develops.

Let's say they misunderstand something. So, they ask a question, and with this understanding they move back to a good translation. But then they feel disturbed by something, perhaps the room is too stuffy, perhaps they don't feel comfortable with a student sitting near them, or perhaps they think about some other thing. Now, when this happens, they are not able to follow what the teacher is saying, or what they are reading in a textbook and another poor translation develops. Perhaps, after a space of time, they are able to lock back into the movement of information and conclude the lesson with some understanding of all that has happened.

Now, this is what a human being does. They drift into and out of the movement of information. How well they are able to keep a good translation is dependent upon how interesting it is for them personally, how they are able to control distractions caused by others, and how well the teacher entertains their mind, rather than just trying to fill it with things they can't relate to.

So, it is vital that students learn how to question when they lose this translation, just as it is for the teacher to keep the mind of their students up to date with each parcel of information from the lesson. We can apply this directly to the student working alone with a task, such as solving a maths problem or writing up an experiment.

The problem is that left alone and without sufficient guidance students so easily go off track. Most have not been taught to constantly check their work, as they progress through it, because of this they end up with the wrong answer, or before the answer, they realise they have lost where they are going.

The problem is that without understanding why they are wrong, and in not knowing what they could otherwise do, they invent the next step. It is this invention when it is created out of inaccuracy, and unclear in how to proceed, that takes them into the realms of error. Once there, it is difficult for them to know how to steer their way to the answer they think their teacher wants.

In other words, the differences in the quality of the answers the teacher receives, which they give a variety of marks to from the top of the class to the bottom, can mainly be caused by their students simply not progressing through their task with a clear understanding of what they are doing, and how they should go about doing this. This all hangs on language."

I pulled down the roller white canvas screen that was positioned over the blackboard and nodded to Jean to turn on the projector. After it had warmed up, I pressed the button on the hand console I had been given earlier for this, and the following image of a teacher and his student came upon the screen.

"As we see here," I began to explain, "the teacher sees the number six, but the boy sees the number nine.

What this cartoon is trying to show us, is that we do not naturally understand the mind of another person, for each understands something through their perspective. It is only through language, the sharing of identities, that a common understanding is gained between individuals. So, we find that language provides the means to decode the definitions of another and the means to develop an awareness of things and the incidents that connect them.

Competence in all this is directly related to the higher sensitivity in the exchange of thoughts as these circulate between the individuals, and the emotional chemistry they share. It is only through this quality of language that a greater awareness to, and so the acceptance for a change of mind occurs.

Thus, when an individual is successful in understanding the information of another, be it verbal, as in discussion or reading as in written, they subconsciously adopt elements of this into the understanding they have of related information, and so the structure by which they can relate to it.

This causes them to change in the strategies they use with information, and in doing so manufacture a change in their mind. Through doing this, they improve in their skill with handling information.

We call this learning. Obviously, the task of the teacher here is to bring the mind of the boy to his side of the table (His world of understanding), so that 'the learner' can understand his mind. This, of course, is what teaching is all about. But by the pressures placed upon the teacher and by a large number of students they have to share their mind with, they are caused to simply broadcast their information and leave it to the developed background, confidence with interaction, and language skills of each student to make their own sense of this.

The responses that the teacher later witnesses to the way they shared their mind, as in how well essays are written or questions answered, are used by them to grade the ability of the students. In the marks and grades that manifest through this, no liability is placed upon the teacher or the environment of the school. The student is simply processed on how well they have struggled to keep up.

Once, we can understand what this means, then we are getting closer to how we can help students gain better grades. And, when we do this, we move away from the excuse that intelligence (And therefore grades) is a product of what the child is born with."

A rather stern-looking man behind one of the tables coughed to clear his throat, and then held up a hand asking me to stop for a moment.

"This sounds all very well," he said, "but we know that students from certain ethnic backgrounds will always perform less well than others."

It was the tone of the word 'less' that I took to mean he was referring to genetic differences, and caused me to reply in this way,

"In the 1990s, I think it was 1994, a book was published called 'The Bell Curve'. This was a very big book. It seemed academic and so to many of presenting trustworthy information, all of which was made more impressive when it was said to be written by two social scientists. The word scientist, of course, conjures up an impression of someone who knows exactly what they are talking about.

It was, then, of no surprise to many that this book set out to prove that intelligence is more or less inherited and that by this African Americans and Hispanics are a whole 15 points below white Americans in intelligence tests. In other words, they are genetically inferior and that because of this they can't get good jobs and are a problem to the American society with drugs, crime and unemployment. The book also warned of the very great dangers that since Hispanic families produce more children than white Americans, that they will create an American population of lower general intelligence."

None of this appeared to disturb this gentleman, although the lady sitting next to him seemed to edge herself slightly to the right and nearer to the woman next to her away from him.

"This book made big news to the general public," I told them. "Yet, what the general public did not know was that other social scientists took the book apart and explained how it was full of false and uncorroborated information. It was, in many senses, just a pack of lies. You can read about this in my second book if you are interested because I discuss this issue in great depth.

But just to show how it was wrong, I want to tell you about a teacher by the name of Jaime Escalante. Now, Jamie was himself Hispanic, and he taught mostly Hispanic children in a poor American school. Year after year, students left this school having failed their final examination or at least with poor grades.

Jamie felt the urge to suddenly change all this. He wanted to give all his students a better chance in life. So, he changed the way he had been teaching and with help from the parents of the students and the students themselves, many of whom were street-hardened criminals, he set about improving their performance.

By effort, inspiration and clear guidelines he pushed, he would not allow anyone to fall behind, the whole class to do better. Their grades did get better, and they got better and better. Now, when the final examination came along and Jamie's class entered these, they all passed. Every single one of Jamie's students passed, and they did so with very high grades. This was unheard of for this school.

So, perhaps naturally, the examination board suspected the whole class had somehow cheated. The entire class was forced to re-sit the examination again because they could not believe that Hispanic students could perform so well in this examination. However, this time each student was placed under personal supervision, to make sure they could not cheat.

Despite the obvious pressure they were under, each of these students managed to produce the same kind of performance they had previously, and earned the same kind of grade. They all passed their finals with very high grades. Jamie had proved that performance, and you can call this intelligence, is not related to people, but to the way those people have been raised to think," – I paused for a moment, before emphasising – "You can never know what the human being can do. After all and further added, the human spirit is far beyond what social scientists think they can measure."

Anyway, this was such a political achievement (In the same way that African Americans made the point in *The Great Debate*) that a movie was made about Jamie and his class. "Has anyone seen 'Stand and Deliver'?" I asked.

There was a hesitant movement before a few hands slowly rose in the air.

"This brings me to a highly important point that we do not realise," I said to them. "From the moment the child entered the school system, they were systemised. In fact, this is and always has been one purpose of school, in that it was to turn undisciplined minds into disciplined ones to conform to the requirements of an ordered society.

But for our concern here, it means that the child's natural inquisitiveness is caged from day one. Oh, we may later try to free it, but it was first caged in order for primary school teachers to control a mass of undisciplined minds and erratic energies. The mind of young children is a mess of scattered thoughts that school requires to operate in tune with that of the teacher's so that all minds march to the same tune. Well, actually, of course, it is the civilisation that demands this of them."

It was Laura who raised a hand to interrupt me.

"Excuse me," she said, "We have laid on a little refreshment, and I can see that it's ready now." She indicated to the door, where we could see a lady standing on the other side of the glass.

"Brilliant idea," I said. All laughed and began to stand up.

I saw the vice principal move down the outer edge of the people attempting to leave the room, before approaching me.

"Well done," he said, "That was most illuminating."

"Thank you," I responded.

Breaks I found were always the time when people feel they can talk to me without disturbing others, and I happily enjoy sharing minds.

"Tell me, what started you off with this passion? For I can understand it is a passion."

"Myself," I replied, "When I was in school I could only ever score marks of 5/10 or 6/10 and thought of myself as average. But when I took my final examinations, I failed every single one. Not a little failure, mark you. I got unclassified for each of the nine subjects I entered. Quite stupid, you know."

He laughed at that.

"So, many years afterwards, I got to thinking. How could my teachers always give me average marks in every class, every week, year after year, but I got no marks in my final examinations after twelve years of school. In fact, it was not that I did not get any marks, but that they said I was too low to give a mark to. I was labelled 'unclassified', and sent out into the wide world."

He looked intrigued.

"Well, with experience of life, I began to realise that the marks the teachers had given me in the class were ones they had used to show their worth. I came to understand then that the marks given out by the teacher only really show how a student varies with others in their class and is not a true indication as to how they compare on a national level."

I looked into his eyes for a moment. He knew what I meant and smiled in agreement after I told him, "They were cooking the books. I mean, if they said I was useless, it would reflect directly upon them. It was the final examinations that proved how useless I really was."

"Or the system," he responded.

Our eyes met. We understood each other.

"And so, I began to wonder what I could have done better when I was in school, and so what children today can do in the ways they actually learn. This is what set me off 20 years ago to study educational, social and political science, plus genetics and neurology. And of course," I added, "how children learn."

"This is highly fascinating. Have you heard of John Holt's book *How Children Fail*?"

"Yes, it's a classic. In fact, I was just going to mention this before the tea arrived."

It was as I said this that I noticed Laura standing by my side holding out a cup and a saucer upon which were laid three ginger biscuits. I love to dunk ginger biscuits into hot tea. The taste is never the same as any other kind of biscuit. I excused myself from Laura and the vice-principal because I needed to organise my thoughts. Soon, people began returning to the room, and so I took my place near the blackboard.

"Before our welcome break," – I gave a warm smile of acknowledgement to Laura (Charlie and his auntie were now sitting by her side) – "we talked about the difficulty of children knowing how to be free with their thinking. As we said, when the child of five or seven begins school, routines are instilled within them. They are told they must do this, and not do that, etc., etc. So, the child learns to understand and to think through rules.

These rules teach the child (Or rather their mind) how to work in school, and also within the academic world. They begin by controlling where the child can sit, who they can sit next to, when they may go to the toilet, when they can move and when they can talk. These rules, then, tell the child how to understand how to learn. They tell them the right way a paper should be placed on the desk, the correct way a pen is to be held, where to place the first letter on the page, and how they should move their hand to draw that letter.

School, just like society, has rules, and how well the child understands from their teacher the value of these rules and when to use them and when they may bend them, conditions their mind. The kids who do better in school, the ones we come to say are more intelligent, are the ones who were better guided to know how to make these rules work.

Rules, you see, also explain how to present a written composition, the ability they have developed to explain their thoughts. So, an older child might get an idea and start to write this down. After a few lines the idea will run dry, and to fill out the number of lines or pages expected of them, they will add spontaneous and often unconnected thoughts until they reach the end.

Now, compare their work with that of another child in their class who was taught to first scribble ideas down and create a goal. Let us say that they were taught how to plan how to start, how to end, and how to lead the reader from one idea to the next with imagination. Their skill in doing this and even their awareness of it is most likely to have been picked up from their parents.

However, at the end of the day 'the system'," (I raised my hands and punctured the air to show quotation marks) "will say one child is cleverer than the other, and as the world of one will become better shaped, so they will appear to continue to be so. Intelligence," I added, "is not to be thought of as to how a child responds, but why don't they respond in a different and better way.

The problem, then, is that once the mind of the child has been so conditioned, not to think freely, and only to do so through the rules each has personally gained knowledge of, we mistakenly have the idea that they should be free in how they think. Now, what really happens here, and this is the crux of all education's problems, is that the child is guided to learn how to think on a model that was devised 150 years ago.

So, school today still teaches children to think in terms of Yes or No. We call this dualistic thinking, rather than using questioning, inquiring and stimulating thoughts from day one. It's true that a movement began in the 1980s, which demanded that children be taught how to be free in their thinking. This sounds wonderful, doesn't it?" I looked around at the expectant faces before me.

"But what really happens is that the free mind is first conditioned not to be free, and then after it has conformed not to be free, it is then told to be free. Simply, the child does not know where the boundaries are and to prevent making a mistake, which is punishable by ridicule from their friends or too many red marks from their teacher, they hold themselves back. When they hold themselves back they limit or restrict their development. This is simply because they do not know how to better proceed. In turn, this causes them to conform to the conditioning that was first placed upon them, and which, of course, enables the school to process them smoothly. This is why today, we still process kids in school, just as we always have done."

I cast a look at the vice-principal, now at the back of the room again and with a nod to him, explained."John Holt wrote about this fear of the child to make mistakes in the 1960s. A very good book to read would be "How Children Fail."

It was interesting to see which of the assembled listeners either took out a pen or borrowed one to write this title down. Indeed, some were making constant notes as I spoke, while others were concentrating on the implications of what I was talking about. All seemed engrossed, for as one teacher would later say to me, "I've never heard anything like this before."

"The problem with all this, then," I continued, "is that when the child (Or student at any age) did not understand a rule as it was introduced to them, and remember here how the mind is always evaluating the world about it, past movies, games to play, a child to be avoided or one to take revenge on, that rule is partially grasped.

When a rule is not completely understood, and the child is then forced to use it, they can only improvise. This is to say that they makeup what they think they should do, which they can only do on the personal experiences they have. So, some students produce better work for their teacher, while others never understand what they do wrong. Think again that from their earliest introduction to school the natural inquisitiveness of the child is crippled, as they are systemised and conditioned by their peers and teachers to be more fearful of asking questions than to enjoy doing so.

From such grounding, each child progresses through their school life influenced in or restrained from asking questions by those around them. With little encouragement to raise an issue and much ridiculed for doing so by their peers, children become fearful of exposing themselves to a mistake. While a very few may raise their hand in response to a question, the very most will hope they never have to, and if pursued will seek to escape with the all too familiar response 'I don't know'."

The problem, then is how can we teach the mind of the student to think freely, after they have been conditioned not to do so for many important years of their official (That is school) development.

As I have just mentioned, later in their school years, they will be encouraged to think more, and we now talk about children being taught critical thinking. Again, we might think that this means that all students are being educated now not to accept information readily and to question it. But the fact is that it is too late in the day for this, and too often it is only brought into aspects of one or two subjects and not given one by itself, where it would better achieve what it is really intended to do.

Therefore, as in all aspects of education, the value lies in the skill of the teacher to be aware of why some children respond to this way of thinking more readily than others, and so to know how to help those who are more passive and are too timid to challenge what they are told. We must remember that confidence is a key issue here.

What is needed is to teach children how to think when they first enter primary school. Not only would this help to equalise the great differences that children were raised on by their parents and so help each to learn better, but it would, in essence, raise the general standard of intelligence. Think not just of five-year-old children in school, or even 12-year-olds later, but the effect this would have when they become working citizens. In fact, this is a key argument I make in the books I have written.

"How could we do this?" It was the voice of the vice-principal, who now had moved closer to me.

"Look," I began, as I sought to provide the answer that I could see many were waiting for, "School is not today what it was when I was a child, yet not much has changed in the ways teachers teach, and how the real worth of the child is understood. There have been surface changes, of course, and many of these, but the basic processing of the child has not.

Still today, students from their earliest beginnings are taught and assessed on the responses they make, with no understanding that intelligence can be taught, or why primary school children should be made aware of how to understand their energies and the corresponding effect of their emotions caused by this. Nor are they taught how to be more sensitive to the world about them. Students throughout their education are not taught how to be more aware of the meaning of information.

May we understand from this that the issue here is not that all children think, but how may they be instructed in ways to think better, after all, the most intelligent race are the European Jews. But as I explain in my books, these people have a very special and culturally dedicated way to raise their children through very clear guidelines in how to understand the worth of information. In this, they are unique."

To explain why I said this, I gave them the following example.

"I was once travelling on a bus, and after a few stops, a family boarded. Now, I often study the way parents interact with their young children while I am travelling. I am always eager to learn new things and to offer suggestions. But I was particularly interested in the way this man took his young son out of the pram and began to play with him. Immediately, he began to play many different kinds of stimulating games.

He would lift his son to allow him to see over the seat in front. Then, he would move him down so he could not see, then he would lift him again. Throughout the whole length of the time they were on the bus, the father was constantly inventing different kinds of stimuli for his son. These were all fun and were all conveyed with meaningful love. But what was of the most significance to me was that the father was very gently singing in Hebrew. I did not know the wording, but I could understand this was an act of transference.

The father was chanting some kind of harmonic melody to his son while he was playing with him, and not, as we may imagine, trying to cause him to sleep. The calm, peaceful learning experience I witnessed here was one this father had obviously been raised on through his culture. Here was a very clear meaning to me of how Jewish children are raised on love and stimulation. As I said, I often watch parents on a bus, but I had never seen anything like this, and yet it was obviously normal for this man.

I would like now to tell you another little but very important story. In America, in the 1930s, there was a superintendent of schools by the name of Mr Benezet. Now, Mr Benezet had the idea that if children learned less but could understand more of what they were learning, then this would help them to think better.

In short, Mr Benezet was trying to find a way to develop their intelligence. He tried out his theory in an area of poor schools, simply because the parents there had less influence in the way the school was run and not much to lose. Mr Benezet chose arithmetic to try out his theory. He did this because he noticed how the way primary school children were taught how to associate numbers was dull and boring and mainly worked on the principle of causing them to copy and reproduce without really thinking of what they were doing. We find this still today, almost one hundred years later.

So, Mr Benezet had the idea of completely removing arithmetic from the primary school's curriculum. Instead of this, young children were taught to reason through relating to stories.

Now, many years later, Mathew Lipman was to achieve great success by building upon this when he wrote his Pixie stories to introduce children to abstract reasoning, learning to work with ambiguity, and how to develop interpersonal relationships.

Accordingly, it was only once Benezet's children had progressed to reach middle-high school that they were introduced to arithmetic and so any form of mathematics for the first time. Now, by the end of that first year and with only this one year of study, Benezet's children were found to demonstrate far greater competency in arithmetic than children who had studied this subject for a number of years.

Of greater significance was the realisation that because they had been taught language skills in the lesson periods when they would otherwise have been taught arithmetic, these children displayed far higher reasoning and ability in language than children who had followed the traditional path and had not been taught these skills.

May it be said, once again, that language is the foundation of intelligence. Understanding the significance of this, Benezet reasoned that the 3 'R's of learning, those of reading, writing and arithmetic, should have arithmetic replaced with recitation. Recitation, however, was not to mean children would recite as we today understand it, but that they should be taught to express their feelings and interests through stories they had learned in their lessons.[11] This need to educate children in reason before they begin to learn the subjects of school are exactly what the pioneer of understanding intelligence, Alfred Binét, believed.

Over one hundred years ago, Binét wrote that children should not first be taught the normal subjects of school, but that they should be given lessons in the will, in attention, in mental discipline. In short, before exercises in grammar, they need to be exercised in mental orthopaedics; in a word they must learn how to learn."

"Incidentally," I explained, "long before I had heard of Binêt or had any knowledge of how school really works, I knew that children needed to understand better they were learning. As I did study how school works and so wrote my first book "The Illusion of Education", so I realized that the reason, or rather the excuse, not to teach children how to reason lay in the belief that they inherit much of their ability for this, and by this being so there is little scope to improve this ability to reason through a subject that would attempt to do so. Once, I really understood how this belief in inherited ability arose as a political strategy, I dedicated many decades of my life to prove why intelligence is not genetically inherited, and therefore why children can learn to reason better if we do have a subject that would teach them this."

It was the vice principal's voice that rose from the silence in the room as I finished saying this.

"Did you say your book was called 'The Illusion of Education'?"

"Well, yes it is. The was the first book I wrote, but then I wrote 'The Illusion of School' to offer practical examples of how teachers and parents can work to improve the learning of students once they understand how it really works. I followed this with 'Intelligence: The Great Lie' to prove why intelligence is not genetically inherited. At least in the way we think it is."

The vice principal was writing as he spoke, but another man, midway in the room raised his hand.

"Excuse me Roy, but the purpose of the genes is to pass on the codes of how to be a human. Doesn't this mean that we do inherit some of our intelligence?"

I liked this man. He was not accusing, but trying to reason intelligently, and I wished I had had more time to answer him properly.

"Thank you," I smiled. "Yes, of course, we have gene codes, but through my work, I came to realise that in an evolutionary sense, our genotype evolved to select the gene codes according to their need.

Thus, codes that enable our physical structure to develop are subject to diversity, so we look different to each other and are attracted differently, which is vital for mating and so reproduction. But codes that relate to our nervous system, and to us, this means the brain of the student, evolved such that genetic diversity does not affect the operation of the features of the brain and the mind, except that is for chromosomal mutations that by example produce Down Syndrome individuals.

Thus, we must have a gene design that enables us to have a mind, but our mind is totally unique to us. It has no genetic relation to the mind of any of our family members other than the codes to enable us to develop it. So, the ways we learn to think and so relate to and react to the world are determined through experience and not predetermined by some genetic quality.

I remember that Fodor suggested something along these lines when he saw how genetic inheritance does not determine how our beliefs can form or does it interfere with our ability to adopt new thinking strategies or our ability to reason freely. Most significantly," – I paused for a moment to give stress to what I was about to say – "Genetic inheritance does not determine our ability to know the language or develop our emotional states. Both of these are constructed totally through our experiences, and both of these incidentally are the deciding factors in how the student is able to relate to information in school and display their understanding of this.

It is also very interesting to point out here, as Flynn discussed, that there has been a surge in intelligence globally over the past few decades that could not be explained genetically. There simply was not an evolutionary time for this to have occurred. This dynamic increase in intelligence could only be explained through accessibility to higher technology, in other words, the environment. So, with all this said and done, and as we readily witness today, any normally born child can be raised to do jobs far beyond the job capabilities of their parents if they have the correct opportunities and guidance to do so. After all, about half of our modern generation go to university from parents who were bricklayers and postmen."

My friend nodded his head in agreement with all I had said, but I could see there were some faces in front of me who seemed a little uncertain to accept what I had just said. After all, I had just overturned everything they and their parents and their grandparents had been raised to believe.

The words of Mark Twain came to my mind as I looked at these good and kind people, 'It's easier to fool people than to convince them they have been fooled.' And I realized after 40 years of research and study into this how our civilisation has been fooled or at least has been unwittingly raised on a political strategy in this. I saw how I needed to give them something they could easier grasp and relate to. So, I took their minds and imagination into the classroom.

"Well, you know," I said calmly, "children in school did not inherit gene codes that determine how quickly and accurately they read the information in a textbook. This speed and accuracy are developed through experience and interest. We select information according to what we feel or think is relevant to us personally. Equally, how we associate this new information to information we have previously stored in our memory banks is reliant upon how well we selected and associated that information to information from earlier experiences and so on and so forth.

All this interaction, although I call it interrogation of information and association, is reliant upon experience. If you wish to go far enough back, I could explain how the visual system in the unborn and neonatal infant becomes formed through experience, because the gene codes for this allow this to happen.

But what we are really talking about when we think of the child in school is how well they understand their lessons. The thing is, is that we really don't know how well they really understand their lessons all we judge them upon is how well they can explain their thinking to us, and this is purely skills in the language.

So, a child who knows the answer very well, but has very poor language skills will not be able to explain very well what they mean and their teacher will give them a lower mark because of this. Equally, if a child does not know the answer, but has developed very high language skills, then, they can present an explanation that would gain them a very good mark, simply because they were able to explain why they did not know the answer sufficiently.

Can you see, school performance simply comes down to language skills and these to the emotional stability of the student as I have just explained? If education would accept this and move out of the tradition that binds it, then we could teach all children how to reason and how to think better through a specific subject for this. So, if we are going to help our children to do better in their lessons, and to be better human beings in their societies, then, we have to teach them how to think.

It's simple really. After all, knowing the answer to a question is very much more than a right or wrong response of ability. That response is merely the conclusion of a long history of very many processing techniques that have developed through experience, opportunity, and desire."

That was the cue to end the evening. I bowed slightly and everyone broke into applause. People stood up and left the room. Some in a hurry, presumably to get back home, others moved slowly as they talked between themselves. The man who had raised this issue of intelligence being related to racial backgrounds gave me a beaming smile of congratulation as he walked past, and paused briefly to shake my hand.

"Thank you for clearing up something that had always niggled me," he said.

Laura and the vice principal held back, and once the room was clear approached to thank me.

"Would you like to come and meet my teachers?" he asked.

My heart exploded with excitement. I love to share my mind with teachers, but much, much more with children. And that is how we started Chapter Two.

Chapter Ten
18-Month-Old Lizzy

The day had not been so busy, which gave me time to sort out some papers and dwell upon a class I had been teaching. The clock ticked away and I had quite forgotten the time when there was a sudden knock at my door. It was opened by Alice, who introduced a lady whom I took to be in her mid-twenties accompanied by a small toddler. The little girl, I was to find, was 18 months old.

"How can I help you?" said I, thinking the mother had come to see me about another child.

"I want Lizzy here to get into the best kindergarten in my neighbourhood," she told me.

Now, I should explain here, that I am very much against parents pushing their children to excel because they fear their child will underperform to their expectations. I have met too many children who 'lost' a happy childhood with problems later in life because they were pushed too hard by a parent. When I looked at this happy toddler who now was running about my office, I felt a need to caution the mother to just let the child be happy.

"If she is happy in life," I said, "and you can guide her in fun activities, (I stressed the word fun) and you bring meaning to these, then Lizzy will be better ready to begin school life than if you try to enrol her on some super early learning course."

"But she has to get into this school," the mother told me. It was almost like a command.

I watched the eyes of the mother and could understand the concern that had built up within her.

"Look," I said, "this particular kindergarten offers you a service. You will have to pay a lot of money for this. It's their business. What would you do if you could not afford their fees?"

"Well, I can't," she responded, "but I have to find the money by working extra hours."

"Don't you think those hours would be better spent with your daughter?"

"Do you mean I shouldn't send her there?"

"I mean that the time your child has with you at this age is very important for her emotional stability. Certainly, she needs to share time with other children, but at her age, she needs the love and security of her immediate family, more than the academic value a kindergarten would give her."

"But what if she doesn't get into the right school?"

How education is a big money machine I thought when I heard this. How parents are brought to concern and some to worry so much they have to borrow huge amounts of money and place themselves in long term debt, for a service that should be equal and free to all parents. But then, I reflected a little sadly, this is not the world we live in, and parents are being unduly stressed to focus on grades when all should be focusing on emotional stability.

"The role of the parents is of great importance in the educational development of their child," I told the mother, "We are cultivated to think that the mother and father create their child, that the parents raise their child until a certain age, and that from that age they turn them over to the school system. This, they are led to believe, will do its best to create the best opportunities for their child.

Schools play on this as each competes against the other to convince you that they are their best place to send your child, and warn you of the consequences if you choose a lesser school. But the greater reality is that the teacher, in any school, does not have the time and in many cases the understanding of how to really improve the academic performance of every single child in their class.

So, in too many senses children are processed in school today as they always have been. What you will more often find," I continued, "is that the better schools or institutions are least so because of their staff or facilities, and more because they attract children who were well prepared for this opportunity by their parents. It is this better behaviour of the class as a whole and a greater awareness of learning, which comes from the parents, that generally enables the teacher to teach better."

Gillian, as I now knew her name, began to seem more relaxed. Lizzy had by now come to her mother and was sitting on her lap.

"Well, what should I do?" she asked me.

I had by now already passed a crayon to Lizzy, who was trying to understand what she could do with it.

"Do you colour with Lizzy?" I asked.

"Of course, I buy her lots of books."

I quickly drew a small number of circles overlapping each other on a piece of paper before me, and in passing this to Gillian asked,

"Could you please ask Lizzy to colour the circles I have marked with a cross?"

Gillian told her daughter to do this, and we both watched as Lizzy proceeded to drag the crayon from left to right in sharp and zigzag movements. There was no fine control.

"Do you know why we encourage children to colour?" I asked.

"Because it's fun for them," the mother responded in a matter of fact manner.

I shook my head. Gently taking the crayon from Lizzy, I rotated it in small circles on the paper to neatly colour one whole circle.

"No, It is to teach them dexterity with finger and hand, to prepare them to better hold a pencil or pen to later write letters," I told her.

I allowed Gillian to see the widely scribbled colouring Lizzy had made, and the neat circle I had coloured in contrast.

"You can begin to show Lizzy, how to hold a crayon correctly and encourage her to understand how she can best colour shapes than just to give her a crayon, a fun picture and congratulate her when she has finished without any guidance."

"But how does this teach her how to write letters?" she asked.

I drew two marks on the paper and gaining Lizzy's attention to what I was doing, drew a straight line to connect them. I drew two marks again, but closer together this time, and asked Lizzy to join them together. I helped her to put the crayon on one mark, and both watched as the crayon shot off in the wrong direction.

"Brilliant!" I exclaimed, "Very wonderful, Lizzy." The child felt a sense of success. I then showed her again, the mark she should have aimed at. This time she was more successful, although went far beyond it.

"Fantastic!" I exclaimed, giving Lizzy encouragement.

"Now, Watch this," I asked Gillian.

Over the next few moments, I drew a number of marks on the paper, gradually increasing from two to four as to form a rough square, and with each step encouraged Lizzy to try to find the marks with her crayon.

I soon handed Gillian a paper with a vaguely drawn circle.

"Now watch this," I said, "as I drew a small dash to the bottom right of the circle to turn it into the letter 'a', then, in making another circle, I added a long dash to the higher left of it, to turn it into a 'b'. I explained to Lizzy which was which and in drawing a new circle, asked her to turn this into an 'a'. Before I had finished talking, Lizzy had placed the dash where it needed to be and giggled as excited small children do.

Over the next few minutes, I taught Lizzy how to draw a 'c' in the same way and then how to draw a 't'. I then gave phonetic sounds to the 'c', the 'a', and the 't'. After we had played with these sounds and letters for a further few moments, I asked Lizzy to write a letter as I pronounced it, which she did and so wrote the word 'CAT'.

"You see," I said to Gillian, "if you can guide Lizzy in slow and clear steps with lots of praise and love, she can write letters at 18 months of age. You have seen how she has just spelt one word. In six months, without any pressure, she should be able to write the alphabet. You can teach your child. Enjoy this experiment with your daughter, and build up for her one of the skills she will be judged upon when she begins the real school."

The mother looked very happy and had a gleam of pride for her daughter.

"Make the time you have to spend, sharing skills with Lizzy. Read her a story every night."

"We do. That is, her father Bill or I do."

"Great, but don't just read from a book. A book is great if it has interesting illustrations, but sometimes, ask Lizzy what she likes and create a little story with her thoughts. Get her involved with it. In the beginning, let her tell you how the story will end. Other times, let her begin the story and then show her how it could develop through your experience.

Whenever you can, get Lizzy involved in the world about her. The more you talk, the more new words you introduce her to, the better she can interpret the meaning of the things she sees. You see Gillian, if you and Bill, and perhaps Lizzy's grand-parents help her to write, to read and to learn how to understand things and most importantly how to always better explain her mind, you don't need to worry about the best kindergarten to send her to.

But what is important is that she mixes with children who will not hurt her too much, so she can learn to have respect for others and to know how to earn this for herself. Don't be sold on 'the best'. Find the best for your child with what you can afford, and what you can do. Remember, at the end of the day, the child's progress through school will much depend upon the guidance they receive from their parents."

After this, Gillian or occasionally Bill would bring Lizzy to meet me. Sometimes, they came just once a month. But as I realized, Lizzy was happy, outward going with friends she had developed, and learning the 3 Rs (We had also begun to teach her simple numbers and their relationships), I saw no immediate need to see her again.

As I came to discover many years later, Lizzy is now in primary school and doing well. She did not go to the most expensive kindergarten, but her parents did manage to create the best way to prepare their daughter for her school life. Unless she encounters nasty children who will try to destroy her life with bullying, she may well achieve all the hopes her parents have for her.

Chapter Eleven
Chris and Little Bell

"Excuse me, Roy," Alice's head appeared as she opened the door.

"There is a rather anxious man come to see you. He can't keep still and is constantly fidgeting.

"It's OK," I nodded. "Please show him in."

I had barely mentioned this when a very large man entered the room, almost knocking Alice out of the way as he did so. He was obviously much stressed, and I wondered what had brought him to me. We introduced ourselves and the man sat down in the chair I offered.

"I can't stop it," he told me with an agitated tone.

"Can't stop what?" I asked intrigued as to what was causing this man such dilemma.

"The bloody Smartphone," he exploded, "Oh, I'm terribly sorry, I'm just so much in a state."

"It's OK," I reassured him, but I knew what he was going to talk about.

As Chris explained, this was the man's name I came to understand; his wife had given their four-year-old a new Smartphone. All were very happy in the beginning. The child, a little girl, was pressing buttons and laughing and sharing things with her mother. But within a very short time, she became reclusive, ignores her mother and doesn't want to play with other children. When the father took the phone away from his daughter, this four-year-old went into a violent rage. He had to give the phone back to calm her down. Now, she just plays with this thing, does not respond when Chris or Wendy, his wife, ask questions and try to share things with her.

"Well, I've heard of ADHD and I'm really worried that my daughter has this. I know they give drugs to kids who have this. I don't want that. I just want my little girl back." The look of desperation was so clear on his face.

I nodded in full understanding.

"I'm sure your daughter does not have this," I said, trying to calm him down. "What is your daughter's name?"

"Bell."

"Chris, what you are experiencing is very, very normal today. So many, I might even say almost all parents today do what your wife did. We want our children to learn and we give them a Smartphone thinking this will help them, but what most of us do not know is how this changes the chemistry in the brains of our children and so their behaviour. This reaction of Bell, when you took the phone away, is very normal. It's nothing to be worried about and I'm sure it has nothing to do with ADHD, but we have to find a way to control her use of the Smartphone."

"How?" he asked.

"Well, the first thing we have to do is to realise exactly what is happening. You see, Smartphones do give out a level of non-thermal radiation, this does disturb our brain activity, but because young children have skulls less dense than ours this radiation affects them more. I'm sure Bell has trouble sleeping."

Chris nodded.

"Lost interest in what she eats," I continued.

"Oh, no!" he interrupted me, "She loves burgers and cakes."

Thoughts of high levels of sugar and low nutrition were beginning to enter my mind. I could imagine Bell in ten years, with the levels of obesity rising in our civilisation and the health problems this child would likely have in middle age.

"One thing at a time," I said to myself, ignoring this remark of Chris.

"Well, many of the games she is playing on the Smartphone will be of a win or lose type. These will seed within her mind a frustration if she does not win one time, and a drive to keep playing until she does win the game. Then, of course, she will be led to the next game and the next. It's a never-ending process that addicts her to the Smartphone. This need to win drives a chemical called dopamine in her brain to overproduce. When this happens, she will become naturally more aggressive. This is why Bell went into a rage when you took the phone away. She simply went overboard when the addiction was suddenly halted."

"My God," his face looked very worried. "But all kids play with these things," he added.

"I know," I replied, "they are a real threat to the development of mankind. Smartphone addiction runs into computer game playing addiction, where our young lose social skills. Their minds only live within the illusion of a game, so they don't develop social skills of interaction. When someone has a problem, they are not interested. They have little compassion, but when they have a problem they don't have the experience of language to know how to explain themselves. So, they get frustrated and angry without any apparent reason. Our children are really living in a very toxic world, we just do not understand. So, this is not just Bell."

A sigh of relief spread over his whole face.

"Well, what can we do?" he asked.

"There are a number of experts who recommend that smartphones should not be given to children under ten or twelve years of age. Kids need time to develop social skills, which these phone games deprive them of. My advice to you is to plan a number of physical activities with your daughter and her friends, talk to their parents about this and get them onboard; plan trips to the zoo, museums, and walks in nature. Have books with puzzles in and books of stories, and paper and pen games to play, so that you are moving their mind out of the 'Win and Not Lose' addiction. Then, create an excuse to stop Bell from having a phone."

"I tried that," he said.

"No, you snatched the phone away. This was an abrupt and very disturbing action to Bell. We have to be more subtle. Something like…" – I was searching for an idea – "…secretly cut the power cable so the phone cannot charge up or some other devious action. We've got to be devious in this with such a young child because she is too young to really reason with.

When the phone is not working, say you will get another but do not. Then, activate your plans to get her mind involved with real-life activities. With a four-year-old, this should be relatively easy. It may not be with older children and then we would need some kind of incentive to cause them to want to spend less time with the phone games for the reward that more interests them. In fact," I added, "we are playing a greater game, a game to win back our children!"

A look of success came into Chris's eyes. He had found a way to take control of the situation, and with this, his fears and stress went away.

A month later, I opened a large envelope on my desk to find a photograph inside of a happy father, a happy mother and a very, very happy four-year-old girl all playing a board game together on the floor. Written across the photograph were the words, "Thank You, All our love, Chris, Wendy and Little Bell!"

The reader will by now be all too familiar with how cortisol can disturb the ability of the student to concentrate on their schoolwork, and so why the processes it puts in motion are important factors in hindering the development of a child's ability to learn.

The following chapter is offered as a model for the teacher to discuss this process with their students, as they seek to dissuade them from bullying. Some readers may wish to move directly to the following chapter.

Chapter Twelve
The Bullied Child

"I was reading your article on bullying in LinkedIn the other day," said the vice-principal, who by now was becoming a much-valued friend.

"Well, actually it was in support of the work that Rusty does," I replied.

"An acquaintance of mine in California, Rusty May, travels around schools talking to children about the reality and the tragedy of bullying. He does a wonderful job, and I was always happy to support him as he struggles to give all children a happier and safer life."

The vice principal was interested to know more about the long term effects of bullying on the victim, and after a little deliberation asked,

"I wonder if you would like to come and meet my students. We have a few bullies and we keep an eye on them, but I am sure you know how devious they can be in their schemes to terrorise."

"I'd be more than happy to. When would you like me to come?" I asked.

"Well, I need to square it with the teacher I have in mind," he said, obviously weighing something up as he spoke.

"Do you mean one class?" I said, "Why not the whole school, a general assembly?"

"Two birds with one stone, eh! That could work very well. Let me talk to the boss about it, and I'll give you a call."

"Fair enough, just let me know."

Nothing happened for over a week, and it was just when I was beginning to think he had forgotten when the telephone rang.

"Could you make it this Friday?" he asked, a little stressed, "The head was away for a few days, and yesterday, well, we had 'an incident'."

The words 'an incident' had a cold almost a bitter tone to them. "I'd like to see what you can do. Would Friday 8.30 be OK?"

An appointment had been cancelled due to the flu, so I was more than happy to come.

So it was, that on Friday at the appointed time I entered the main assembly hall, after a brief meeting with the headteacher.

When I stood upon the small stage, after I had been introduced, I looked down at the 1,000 students and remembered how it was for me when I stood in the assembly hall. The floor then was wooden, and I remember being lined up by our class teacher, each boy quickly rubbing the front of his shoe against the back of his sock, in a somewhat desperate attempt to look smart. The headteacher we had was not as gentle as this man seemed; a huge and terrifying man to any boy. He always wore a cloak and mortarboard, and always, I mean always, carried a cane in his hand. He was, it may be imagined, never slow to use it, and to be called into his office was as good as a death sentence to us then.

Thinking of him now brings a memory back. We were playing in the schoolyard after dinner, and as ever curious as children, we found a window slightly open in a shed behind a building. With any excuse to innocently explore, we climbed in through the window.

There was little to interest us except for a bowler hat, which my friend Chris found lying in a box. He placed it on his head and acted the part of Charlie Chaplin. Another friend crept up behind him and pulled the brim of the hat down over his eyes. The brim came off! Chris just stood there, with a funny Stan Laurel smile. He was always happy to play the clown. We all laughed that is until I lifted the now destroyed hat off his head and looked inside. There, in bold ink, was the name of the headteacher. I never knew how we got out of that shed so quickly, but we did and disappeared as if we had never existed.

Still, that was of a different time, and the children facing me now could not be imagined to even think about polishing their shoes. Most, anyway, wore sneakers.

I looked about and welcomed them all.

"I once met a young man," I began, (A start that was not expected, for I knew the children thought I had come to lecture them and not tell a story, but stories open up our heart and invite us to dwell upon a meaning they contain.) "He was working in a bank, and as our conversation developed he asked me what I did. I thought," I told them with a joking tone, "that he would ask me why I was so broke."

The hall fell apart with laughter, students and teachers alike. This was exactly what I needed, relaxed minds, willing to listen.

"But fortunately for me, he just wanted to know my job. Well, I told him I wrote books about how children learn and, well, sometimes, I can help in a school. I also mentioned that I wrote about bullying. Now, the moment I mentioned the word 'bullying', there was a brief silence between us. I could tell something had happened to him because the next words he spoke were a little jittery."

"That happened to me. I was bullied at school," His voice was low when he told me this, and judging by his age I guessed this must have happened about ten years ago.

"I still think about it now. Almost every day, I think about that bully," His hands started to shake.

"Now, I can't tell you the details he then related to me, but I was able to help him see things from a different perspective, which gave him some peace at that moment. The problem for this man was not that the bully did not exist anymore, but that his mind had so expected the bully's presence in school that it had altered the way his brain worked. What I want to explain to you today will require you to switch on a little, because I am going to tell you what happens in the brain of the victim and in the mind of the bully.

Our brain (Well at least the part that does the thinking) is not a solid thing like other organs in our body. It's actually formed by a fine myelin sheet that is highly convoluted. This sheet has brain cells growing inside it and makes a lot of chemicals, which we call neurotransmitters. You see, brain cells do not touch each other. They are separated by a tiny gap, and it is the neurotransmitters that carry the signal from one cell to another. Does anyone know the name of a neurotransmitter?" I asked aloud.

"Dopamine!" shouted a voice from somewhere in the middle of the hall.

"Great," I laughed. "Then, this story is going to be very easy. Well, we have about 50 neurotransmitters, and dopamine is a very important one as my young friend out there told me. But there is another, and this one is well, kind of special. You see this neurotransmitter is called cortisol. Can everyone shout 'C O R T I S O L' back to me?"

The word came back to me in one very loud wave. But I held my hand to my ear and pretended I did not hear it.

"What did you say?" I asked, acting both a little deaf and a bit stupid.

"CORTISOL!" The word hit me about ten times louder this time. I smiled at the children, knowing they were likely to remember it now.

"Well, you see...," – and here I acted a little simple to gain their interest. I did not want to appear to be a boring lecturer to these kids – "when the mind gets a bit stressed like you do when a bully says they are going to hurt you, or when someone tells others something nasty about you, well, the brain makes more cortisol than it normally does.

As the cortisol level goes up, it causes some parts of the brain to work better, but other parts not to work so well. You see, cortisol is there to make sure your brain deals with an emergency, and so it makes the mind think about what is causing this emergency. So, if a lion suddenly came into this room," I shouted and pointed sharply to a doorway, upon which most turned their head for a brief moment, "your brain would want to think 'How fast can I get out of here?' Then, you would not be interested in listening to me, would you?"

"No!" The word came back as a chorus.

"Exactly!" I said laughing. "So, you see this is what happens when you are learning. When you are happy, well as happy as you can be in school," I grinned. "The parts of your brain that work with working things out, analysing, trying to find answers, that kind of thing works very well. But when you get bullied, your mind causes the cortisol level to go shooting up and you can't think anymore about trying to find an answer. All your mind is now doing is thinking about the bully. The problem," – and I winked to them here – "is that when the mind thinks the bully will come again, it causes the brain to produce the cortisol it thinks it will need.

So, even though the bully might only be present for a few minutes, the fear in the brain of the victim is causing so much cortisol that they can't concentrate on much else for a long time afterwards. They can't think about the lessons they are doing. They can't think much about the homework they have to do. Now, the problem for this young man in the bank was that he never stopped thinking about that bully. Oh, the bully had long since gone on his evil little way, totally unaware that what you give out ALWAYS comes back to you."

At this moment I spoke very seriously to them, "It always comes back. What you give out comes back. If you give kindness, kindness returns," I did not state the obvious, because I wanted them to think about the word kindness.

"So, the bully did not understand how he had destroyed this young man's life. Every day for ten years, he was nervous and not happy. Who wants to be happy here?" I asked them.

Most put up their hand.

"Is that all?" I asked.

I looked to a boy who was bigger than the rest, "Would you like to be happy?" I asked him.

He nodded briefly.

"Well, put up your hand," I told him.

He did not. I suspected he could have been a bully.

"Come on. Hand up. Help me," I raised my hand.

Slowly, his hand rose.

"Great!" – I looked around – "Come on, is there anyone here who does not want to be happy? If so leave your hand down."

There was a shuffling sound and all had a hand in the air.

"Good!" I told them. Oops, there in the front row was a small boy holding both hands down but wearing a huge grin. The joker! I laughed with him and managed to shuffle both his arms up. After that, every single child in that hall wanted to be happy. Now, they knew it.

My tone changed. It became kind and sympathetic.

"Now, we all have problems with others. Sometimes, we don't like them because they did something to hurt us. Sometimes, we don't like them because they look different to us. I was bullied because I wore glasses. But you know, no matter what another looks like on the outside; they are just the same as you on the inside. They just want to be happy.

So, next time you think you want to hurt someone or say something nasty about them, you have got to realise that you are changing the chemicals in their brain, if they let you. Now, I don't know if you personally believe in God. I do. I love God. Maybe you are not sure and you think about the Universal Mind. Maybe you don't think about it. But I want you to know," I spoke very seriously now, "I want you to know that whatever you do, good or bad, will come back to you.

So please think, think very carefully if you really want to cause pain to someone else, because as sure as the day is light and night is dark, that pain will come back to you. Oh, it might not come back in the same way, but one day someone will do something that will cause you a lot of pain. When this happens you will shake and feel frightened. You might have nightmares. But sometime later, you will see for yourself that 'this is like I did to him or to her'. It always comes back. A baddie never has a happy life.

So, I want you to STOP and THINK, do you really, I mean really want to give someone such unhappiness, maybe for all their life. Be careful, be very careful, when you answer because if you do, you can't escape what is going to happen to you."

I stopped speaking for a moment. I wanted them to absorb the meaning I had just given.

"Now, with this young man in the bank, I told him that if he learns to meditate, he will physically lower the cortisol level in his brain, and he will then not think more about that bully. He will be happy with his thoughts and do his job better. Whenever the ghost of that bully appears, he just has to relax, meditate for a moment, shrink that bully into a very, very insignificant size, which is what the bully is really frightened of, and he will be free, completely, completely free. So, if there are any bullies amongst you, I am sorry, really sorry for what is going to happen to you.

For the victims," – I looked around with a warm kind smile – "learn to meditate. Learn to be free. Don't let the bully be bigger than they want to be, because you are far, far bigger than they are, which is why they are frightened of you. Don't you know this?"

My time with the assembled school had come to a close. The headteacher came on to the stage, shook my hand and asked the assembled students to thank me, which they did. Wholeheartedly, I may add.

Chapter Thirteen
A Class in Learning

There had been some small articles about the changes I was trying to bring into education in a local newspaper. One of these reached a national paper, and it was on account of this that I received a telephone call from the headteacher of a large school.

He explained to me that a teacher had just taken maternity leave, and he would like me to replace her because he wanted to bring new ideas into his school.

I began very shortly after our conversation and found that as I entered the school, met children and was introduced to teachers, that the school environment was not very different to that in which I had been educated 30 years earlier. It was not, of course, the same, but it was not notably different either.

The lessons I was invited to watch reminded me of that distant time when I had sat in the rows before my teacher, although now the environment of the class was more cheerful. The walls were painted with brighter, happier colours, and decorated with colourful illustrations made by the students themselves. Yet, all in all, not very much was different to my time as a student. Indeed, the way the teachers taught did not seem that much different either.

Each stood at the head of their class just as visible and tangible and yet totally detached from the hearts and minds of their students. They spoke for a while, made some illustrations on the blackboard (Which those near the back of the room could not clearly see), and from this introduction referred their students to work from page 44 to page 49 in their textbooks.

One or two students would raise a hand, and the teacher would move to answer the question that was asked. Students talked among themselves, the teacher shouted, the students stopped talking but after a respectful pause started whispering. Those who were using mobile phones discreetly under the desk continued to text messages to each other.

The time moved through the lesson, the air was stale, and the children were thinking of the refreshments they could buy in the break. That break suddenly came, when all had thought the bell had forgotten to ring. When it finally did, books closed, bags were slammed on desks, and while one or two struggled to push their book into a bag that had no space, the rest of the class had disappeared as if they had never been there.

The teacher went around, collected the homework books left behind and carrying these under their left arm, moved through the door out into the corridor and towards the teachers' room.

When it became my turn and I entered each of my classrooms, I tried to be what those students desired of a teacher. I reasoned that they wanted someone who was as similar to their idea of a mentor as the age difference between us would allow. To 8-year-old insecure and excitable children I was a caring and admirable father figure. To 16-year-olds who were apathetic or resentful to all that their privileged world had provided for them, who sat defiantly clad in woollen hats and thick overcoats in a warm classroom, objectionable in every possible manner to the authority they did not understand, I was a university of life adventurer.

When I first walked into the classroom of these adolescents, my environment was already stereotyped. My chair and my desk were waiting for me, placed there to endorse the authority I was endowed with. So, they stood cold and forlorn at the head of columns of smaller desks and littler chairs. Yet, this was the very thing that separated me from the freedom of the minds I sought to reach. By some means, I had to become the same as these youths but respected as their guide. It was to be a place I had to earn.

The first thing I had to do was to dispel the contempt they held for their idea of what school meant. Yet, I wanted to do this as a part of them and not with any sense of commanding authority. Accordingly, in the first lesson and to their wide-eyed amazement and undisguised amusement, I sat on the floor. As I made myself comfortable, I coerced them to come and join me, for to get them away from their seats and desks, which they saw as their territory, was to get them to surrender a small part of their resistance. We met in no man's land.

In that first lesson, I told them to put away the textbooks they had automatically pulled out of their bags, and I ignored the lesson plan. Instead, I told them stories of my life; whom I had met, what I had gained from these people, where I had travelled to, and what I had done. We all love stories. It is a part of human nature, and (As I have said many times in this book) so we can learn best through the presentation of a story. That is if, it is told in the way we desire to hear it.

The thing about education is that it takes students and tells them what to learn, without explaining to them why they are learning this. So, while I was able to fuel a purpose in their life through my experiences, and so encourage their need to take this chance of education seriously, opportunities after school became more realistic. As the world opened up in their minds, so the purpose and meaning of the subjects they were studying made sense.

You can't be a doctor; I told them if you do not want to learn the Periodic Table because you have to really understand how the chemistry of the body works. Nor can you be a good manager if you don't know history. History is far more than knowing when the Second World War started. It's to really understand the lives of people before this and how social events brought it about. Any battle, any famous person in history is only a key to begin to understand why it happened or how it came to be.

"You all know about the American Revolution or The War of Independence, but do you know why the British call it one and the Americans the other?" I asked them, as I began to awake in them an understanding of collective thinking and so politics.

Then I asked, "So, you have heard of the American Revolution but have you heard of the French Revolution?"

"Of course," I was told from many in the room, "We had to watch Les Misérables," they told me.

"But this movie or the novel by Victor Hugo has nothing to do with the French Revolution," as I said this, many moved in their chairs, a little puzzled even curious.

"In 1830, the people of Paris became fed up with their life under King Charles X. A new king was elected by the people, but after two years life was no better than it had been before. The people were burdened by heavy taxes, and as the income gap widened between rich and poor, the lifestyle of the poor deteriorated. Then, a cholera epidemic hit the city and brought a severe economic crisis.

At this time, a hero of the people who argued for better human rights and political liberty, General Lamarque died of this dreaded disease. As the people, nearly 100,000, came to pay their respects, a fight broke out between activists and loyalists. Within moments, the whole of Paris was up in arms against their new king, and another revolution had begun. This was in 1832, and this was what Les Misérables was about."

Their eyes widened. All had seen the movie. All had seen the part of the fighting about Lamarque's funeral procession, but none understood why. All were thinking of the wrong revolution. "Knowing dates," I told this class, "is important to relate the event to the causes that brought it about. So, don't just learn dates like you did the multiplication tables. Learn the events behind those dates and you will uncover many hidden mysteries. History," I explained, "is alive. It's a way you can understand your life through the people who lost theirs."

So, I gave reason and explanation as to why they should try to be better with grammar in their language lessons because this gives life to feelings and expressions, which is the essence of being human. Learning physics was given new light, when I blackened out the room, lit candles, and described how Edison struggled through 3,000 filaments before he was able to bring light to the world.

"Without Edison," I told them as I suddenly switched on all the lights and temporally blinded them, "there would be no television and no computer games!"

I brought the curriculum to have relevance in their lives. This gave purpose to why they had to come to school. I told them how they controlled the grades they got, and how by paying better attention and questioning things they missed or did not understand, their dreams could be more possible.

I did not tell them about the politics of education and why all could never obtain top marks. But I did give substance to my claims that their grades were not 'just' decided by the teacher, by explaining in simple terms how the brain works.

As they understood the need for sensitivity and greater awareness, unknown realms opened up and they began to examine information more sensitively and then to check for errors more frequently. As they came to see how they held their grades more in their own hands than they had realized before, the fantasy world of computer games in which they lived faded in relevance.

"Education is real," I told them, "Don't waste time or be distracted from the opportunity your great grandparents never, never had and could not even dream of. You hold the world in your hands; make it a better, kinder, happier place to live."

So, I explained how we would work as a team. I explained that I wanted them to give me their full concentration for about 10 to 15 minutes at a time, and in between, they could relax and have their time. I explained that this was because their brain could only hold attention for a limited period, and how it then needed time to reassess what it had taken in before it was ready for further information.

When I shortly came to teach them, I always tried to 'feel' for the time of a break. I told them they did not need their textbook, because I would tell them what was in it in a way they could understand, and that we would make every point understandable as much as possible in 'our' language. I wanted to develop a language that was common to all of us, and which helped children from diverse backgrounds to keep up. In essence, we would learn by doing.

I told them that for their brain to be active, it needed a supply of fresh air and energy. To enable them to acquire these, I told them they could move about the classroom while I taught, but that they would have to learn from each other the respect they would have to give while doing so.

I allowed them to behave as adults and told them of the consequences if they failed that trust. I told them we would learn new things, and that their brain would get tired of keeping up with all the changes we examined if it did not get the nourishment it needed. So, as the lessons began, they sensibly learned to eat sandwiches and chocolate while they scribbled down notes, for I well knew that many of them came to school without any breakfast. If a car is to go it needs fuel. The brain is no different. I taught them to have respect for their environment by making them search for any crumbs, paper or mess they made while eating.

I treated my students like adults, and they responded in this way. I wanted to explain to these young people why they were in school in a way they could understand, and what their time in this might mean to them for the rest of their lives. I was sure they all knew it meant they would go to work, but the beauty of this opportunity lay hidden from them. When they entered the classroom for their second lesson, they were taken aback. The ordered desks they had come to know as their bastions of defiance had disappeared. Instead of desks laid out in rows facing the blackboard, all the desks were now set around the back and the two sidewalls to leave an open space, facing the blackboard.

However, fitting into their chairs was a bit of a squeeze at first for the students, because the room was not designed for this, but it worked. Now, I could stand in the middle space and by turning my head and moving my body I had direct contact with each and every single student instantly. I had the ideal stance for mediation, the means of helping their mind to better understand mine through constant dialogue.

Eye contact is one of the most important strategies in teaching. As the old saying goes, 'You can't teach, unless you can look into the eye of the learner.' By being able to read a student's eye movement, the teacher gains a very good impression of how easily the mind of the student is handling their information, and also the desire of their heart to want to engage with it. This gives the teacher fine control over the direction they should take with the lesson at any one moment. By this control, they may either carry on with their plan or hurriedly scrap it and invent a new means to share their message.

The traditional layout of rows and rows of desks does not provide this means of eye contact, and by the distance, they manufacture between the students and their teacher they actively hinder the act of learning. Yet, nearly every classroom I walk into, in any country of the world, America, Australia, England, Romania, China, still uses this 19th Century basic design; not all, of course, but the very, very most still do.

The educational planners today do not know or understand the politics behind education, and so why this classroom of desks is as it is, and why children are not taught how to think once they begin their school life.

With desks arranged in the manner I illustrate here, I could leap to any student at any instant, and move to any student with total freedom. This meant that I had the ideal opportunity for direct mediation. This is the only design of a classroom that I have found that makes it possible to employ the technique that is so necessary for successful teaching with one teacher and 30 students at the same time. The design of the classroom in this way also meant that none of the students could afford to be distracted by other thoughts, students, or mobile phones, because the teacher is omnipresent in their mind.

By this means of mediation, I was not an isolated authoritative figure in the distance. I was a human being who had feelings, understandings and concerns, because as I could read their eyes so could they read mine and knew who I was.

As one student inclined their head to one side in puzzlement it was a signal for me to go at a slower pace and keep my eye on them, as I followed the expressions of others in the class. With this understanding, it would have been negligent of me as a teacher to stand by the blackboard, and in trying to educate my students, ask them after 30 minutes if anyone had any questions. I knew that if I did this, the most prominent question in their minds would most likely be "What is this all about?"

When I sat the students of my class in the open desk arrangement, which I suggest that every teacher uses, they found it was easier to directly interact with me. This gave them the confidence they needed to ask questions and for me to give immediate and accurate responses.

This way, all the students could see how it was easier for them to keep up with the lesson content. By helping them to realise I had made it easier for them to learn, so they thought of me as more of a friend, which enabled me to help them more with the personal problems that were distracting them from their learning. This is what teaching is really about. It is not just giving information, but learning to reach the heart of your students to help their mind to keep order with all that is happening.

I should explain here that I encouraged one school to use this layout, which they did, but I was disappointed to find teachers sitting behind their desk now placed in the middle of the room. This is not the meaning here. If learning is to be alive, then so must the teacher be, and they cannot do this sitting down. There should be no chair for the teacher to sit upon in this classroom design. The teacher has to be on their feet, alive, interactive and fully stimulating the minds of their students as any actor or actress on a stage. In the very simplest sense, this is the key to improving education.

Accordingly, when I taught and described information to my students, I used drawings and sketches as much as I could do instead of giving too many words. Words, of course, are vital, but the idea was to enable all the students (with different minds) to have the ability to lock more easily into the information I was sharing with them. This was how I formed our language.

True to my word, we seldom used textbooks. Whatever was in the textbook for that lesson I learned beforehand and explained it to them in 'our' language. It was my job to know that information and to know it inside out, not just to know the page it was on. I wanted them to learn through discussion, not just by relating to what another had written, and to this aim, I strove to get them to disagree and to question information instead of receiving it passively.

So, I told them the story for each lesson, and I juggled significant points with illustrations, fascination and amusing accounts, endeavouring to create my own 'classroom of inquiry'. By yo-yoing from one student to another, as this classroom design allowed me, I endeavoured to show how each could find the link they did not see. Yet, I knew that while I was attending to one, others desired my time at the same moment. While the problem of one may be complex and that of another simple, unless each gains the happy clarification they need they can fail to recognise all the links by which they gain a complete understanding.

It has to be remembered that what every student seeks is not just the piece of the puzzle they miss, but the time to share human feelings and gain acceptance of the identity they are building for themselves into the information. When all are gained, there is a purpose to discovering mysteries and unravelling them. Without all elements, the only purpose is to remember details, because this is what is asked of them. So, as I moved about giving and receiving thoughts, I had to be ever watchful of tired eyes or eyes that told me they were too lost. When these appeared, we took a break.

We worked hard, rested, worked hard, and rested. I tried, as much as possible, to regulate their exposure to information to fit in with the fluctuations of their energy and concentration. With each rest, we played mind quizzes about the content of that lesson and previous lessons, so they could see the relevance of a lesson development. I had to remind them of this, because I knew that too many would have forgotten what happened last time, at least with the detail I needed from them. Every lesson was ended with a quick quiz centred on the most important point of that lesson, with the end lesson of every week having a short fun test.

Everybody liked this test because once they realized that it was for their benefit, and not about me marking them, they wholeheartedly engaged in it. It was more like a paper exercise game. Yet, it told me what they had learned, and it told them what they needed to learn. So, I informed them that if they scored high enough with each test I would not give them homework, because I would know they were up to date with the information I had given them in the lessons to that point. This was the greatest incentive, and it helped to keep the information in the lesson alive and relevant for them.

When I had first entered this class nobody was interested. They were slouched in their chairs totally apathetic to the proposed lesson. On the first test, I gave them the average score was 59%. Six weeks later, they all greeted me when I entered the room. We laughed and joked with each other, they had not needed homework, and the average in the test at that time was 83%.

The point here is that learning in education tends to develop in patches, some with gaps and some overlapping. The point and the problem is that understanding does not develop in small secure and consecutive steps for most of the students. This is because, in the real world of learning, students miss lessons or some aspects of those they attend as they are pre-occupied with a personal problem, distracted by a greater interest, or lack concentration by seeing no relevancy to one point and so miss the one that follows.

It is for this reason that I try to incorporate a high degree of repetition in my lessons. This is an essential practise. Not in the sense of strict repetition, for this would not be stimulating and be counterproductive, but by disguising the appearance of this information and presenting it through frequent and short quizzes that bring new insight through the play of different associations.

In the teaching situation, I have just related, I found that teaching by mediation had made it easier to allow the students to control their own rate of learning. They understood more, and through this, each found their own purpose to the lesson and planned their own use for it. They had wanted to be actively engaged, and this opened up factors for association and so recognition, which meant that each had a higher quality time in the lesson.

To keep up with the flow of information, I taught them how to make effective notes, and how to keep this information alive by reconstructing it through different experiences. Each lesson was taught through discussion, question, discussion and re-question. I painted landscapes in their minds but allowed each to construct the hills, trees, rivers and life that brought relevance to them. So, I taught these students how to monitor information by constructing a theme chart, which linked each point as it was raised, and how they could question information as it became vague or not clear to them.

As we worked as a team, I taught them:
- to be more respectful of each other, with an understanding of how hurtful remarks can disturb the learning process for both.
- why I needed their attention to help them.
- to stop and think before they engaged information, to evaluate it fully, and move methodically through their interaction and presentation of it.

- to be wary of trusting information, and always to be suspicious of it.
- to check and recheck their work, before they give it to another to be evaluated.

In short, they learned how to readjust themselves continually to the flow of information to become a living part of it. The only thing I demanded of them was freedom of their mind, and I knew that to obtain this their minds had to feel unrestricted, trusting, energetic, and intriguingly stimulated.

Incredible things happened. Apathetic and resistive teenagers became students with challenging minds, responsible to themselves and each other. From this, it was always rewarding to see how, when one or two thought to push the limits of freedom and trust beyond the boundaries I had set how they were pulled back into line by their classmates, and not me. As they worked as a team, instead of resenting the success of each other and with some desiring to emotionally or physically abuse another, the general performances moved up the score rating. They looked forward to helping each other. Former bullies became respected friends, which is often what they most desired.

I showed these students a new way of teaching, and how the image of a teacher instructing from behind a desk, conveying a long, boring and meaningless lesson in which students are forced to listen passively and become susceptible to distractive thoughts, could be replaced by a lesson time of mental adventure.

I showed them how teaching through mediation was a lesson raised on questions and conveyed through questions, which stimulates a recognition in each student for the information shortly to be presented to them. By this process, they do not have to struggle to find their own relevance to information, because that relevance has been stirred before the information is presented. So, new information is more readily matched to vague concepts of it in their memory, and greater significance is gained through this. In turn, this fuels their imagination to see possibilities and purpose.

As I think back on those students, now some 20 years ago, I can still see how they were when I first entered their classroom and how so very different they were by the third lesson. They just needed a teacher who was one of them, a friend but a wise one and not a teacher who used authority because they did not know how to be fun and control them at the same time.

Chapter Fourteen
Times of Artificial Intelligence:
Not what you think

I had taken a small group of university students on a trek into the mountains. It was late, one evening, when I and Jack sat by the log fire in a mountain house. All the other students had by now retired to their rooms.

And so, I and this student now sat by the fire, watching the flames escape from the log slowly turning black in the fireplace. I thanked Jack for the mug of hot chocolate he had passed to me. We had been talking about education, and so when he returned with his drink and mine, he asked my thoughts on this topic.

"Well," – I said slowly and with a little deliberation – "if we are to look after students, we first need to look after teachers. We have to give them purpose and energy for the job they are to do. After all, they need this to inspire the hearts and organise the thoughts of our young today, which is not an easy task. The youth of today live in troubled and distractive times, which we little understand. The world was far simpler when I was a child.

Of course, we try to help them and we focus on addiction to game playing, because this is the most obvious to us. But, there are very many other distractions and worries that play on the minds of our young. Peer pressure can be a serious concern to boys and not just to girls. Fashion, as a way of expressing your identity and showing you are acceptable, can be a psychological minefield. There has always been bullying in school, but now it can be more rampant and soul destroying."

As I said this, I was reminded of the greater psychological pressures facing all involved in education.

"Unfortunately", I added, "too many teachers are exhausted, in fact, drained by the administrative tasks and restrictive finances they have to work with. Not to mention the constant meddling of politicians who are always trying to offer a new solution to the public to show they have found the way for a better education, when they have never understood what is really wrong in the first place.

So, examinations, means of assessment, are changed like the weather, which throws syllabus's into chaos, causing teachers to struggle to invent new ways to reexplain to students what most of them did not understand in the first place. All of this is causing teachers to leave education at a worrying rate, especially in a time when the child population is increasing.

What is less seen though, is that this lowering of availability in human teachers will encourage accountants in education to seek ways for children to learn through software programs. Replace the human teacher with an android! Of course, rapid developments in A.I. are making this more and more likely. I think it is enviable that we will see students in the future learning completely through software tasks and similarly evaluated with no human teacher. After all, there are huge savings to be made by replacing a human teacher with a software program. It kind of makes you wonder how many teachers will actually be teaching in thirty years time, perhaps even in ten with the way things are going.

You know, I feel a little concerned that teachers do not realise how they are being slowly phased out. I mean, a school that employs 150 teachers today may well employ twenty in thirty years, and these will not be there to teach. The whole learning process will be governed by software. You can see this coming now. So, teachers who are employed in a school in such a time, may well function not as actual teachers but more as classroom advisors or supervisors to maintain order. After all, with students learning from computers, classrooms in the future may hold 100 or even 150 students in a lesson. In fact, the whole idea of the teacher and the classroom may well change beyond all recognition."

I thought pensively for a moment, before stating, "But it needs to change - and not for this reason."

I watched the flames twisting in the heat above the log.

"You see, the purpose of school and the whole idea of learning is rooted in a 19th century political design. Forget about theories that have sought to help children learn better. The fundamental process has not changed. No matter what ideas psychologists or educationalists come up with to help children learn better, we still have the same variation of performance in a class. One or two understand everything. One or two don't seem to understand anything and the rest struggle in-between pretending they know more than they do.

Today, we think of school as a modern learning environment, but this is a facade that covers how it still works to the design that came out of the Industrial Revolution. This was to create two classes of citizen. One to manage and one to be managed. Social changes and new technologies that have come about since that time have shuffled the ratio of this, but not the underlying means by which education processes its students. We don't see this today and think that all children have equal opportunity in school."

"They don't?" he queried me.

"Well, social programs have helped to make it appear so, but the underlying process by which school works still helps children who were raised with better language skills, instilled with mental stamina, coached to find their purpose in what they have to do and raised with determination to succeed, do better than children lesser prepared by their family.

The home really does make far more of a difference than most realise in a child's schooling. After all, children do not start school equally and the differences made for their preparation at day one often hold right throughout their education. So, the same families tend to achieve similar results in education and go to occupy similar roles in work and society."

"I don't think so," he responded. The whole social sphere used by like this, but it has changed. Any child can gain the right to go to university today and make a better future for themselves."

I looked approvingly. "To some extent this is true Jack, but we need to see the bigger picture. Society realized the need for higher educated workers as our technology advanced and so more universities and colleges were built. To fill these, they had to lower their entrance standards, because school was still producing the same quality of output. School students were little understanding what they were being taught and so gaining lower grades than the university demanded. To facilitate this new design of more going to higher education, school examinations were made easier, just as the standard of entrance to higher education was lowered. All this gave and still gives the impression that children are learning better in school and so that 'any child can now go to university'.

But this image conceals what is really happening, because school children are now not taught to really understand what they are to learn and instead tutored on how to pass examinations. So, they learn 'strategies' to pass the examinations now made easier for them, but very few really understand what or why they have learned these facts. In fact, most students today would not be able to pass a simple school examination of 100 years ago."

"But, we learn to find information in school now, not to really understand it."

"I know Jack, but you have to think of how the mind is developed. Again, look at the bigger picture. …. Learning to understand information and knowing how to find it creates different mental processes. The first develops critical awareness of the value of information. You understand what something means by the value of other information you test it against. The second may be said to develop a searching mind, but in reality this means students learn how to find information through processes of elimination. The problem to this is that when they eventually find the information they are looking for, they immediately accept its worth, because their enquires zeroed into this. The point is that they are not taught to question the validity of their search, by further searching for conflicting or alternative accounts. There is a purpose to this."

Jack looked at me questioningly.

"As I mentioned, you really need to come out of the picture to understand how the mind of the citizen was shaped by their learning process in school. Basically, the average citizen is prepared, by the way they were taught to think in school, to generally accept the information the media presents to them, rather than to question it. In other words, politicians tell the media what to tell the people what they are to think of and so believe, so they support the policies of the politicians. The greater truth is that the politicians are often puppets to powerful interests the public does not see and who really control the events of their lives. This is one" I put emphasis on the last word, "of the factors and purposes of school very, very few know of.

So, when we think of all children being given equality in education, we really have to look a lot deeper to see what this actually means, which is a watering down of the quality of learning in school and so a lowering of the effective mental development of the citizen to be. But, remember also that the opportunity of a university education is not free. This places a restriction on the social wealth of the family, which erodes the idea of equality in education. It comes down to what you can afford to pay for.

"But, we can get student loans to fund ourselves through university."

"Yes, but think how the banks and the whole educational industry thrives off this and don't forget you will spend many, many years of your working life paying off this loan. It is not free and there is a hidden stress associated with this …. If you really want to understand education, you have to see how it works in underdeveloped countries, because there the old social tier system openly determines the opportunities of children according to the work and social roles of their families. Here you find the true purpose of school and indeed education as a whole."

"Well, I think A.I. is changing this."

"Yes, it is absolutely! But school is not changing in the way it should do to accommodate the need that is really beginning with A.I. We have just seen how schools are likely to replace human teachers with computers. Way back in the 1990s, this would have meant computers programmed by human beings. Today, it means computers likely to be programmed by A.I."

I thought for a moment, undecided if I should go down the path my mind had long thought of.

"Well," I said slight with hesitation, "A.I. presents a far, far great danger than people realise."

"What do you mean?" Jack looked at me slightly puzzled.

"Stop thinking of the technological advantages of A.I. and look at the real meaning behind it. Remember, fundamentally we must look at how a society works. We are caused to think of financial wealth, but the real issue is in the mental wealth or rather mental health of the society, for this determines how well it succeeds and indeed if it survives.

"Look," I told him, "it used be said that by 2050, A.I. will take over half of all jobs."

"Ah, but new jobs will be created, so people will still have work," he countered.

"This was the thinking, but developments in nanotechnology have brought a whole new perspective to this. Now we are thinking, and indeed already have prototypes, of machines that can construct any desired product and automatically renew worn parts. The idea that new jobs will be created to replace jobs set about our existing technology, when A.I. replaces this technology, is becoming less and less tenable and this is going to change the whole purpose of school."

"Why so?

"Well, originally school was about instilling the moral and social rules of the society into children, so as adults they would behave as their society required of them to uphold its work ethics and social harmony. Learning was a slightly secondary factor in this design. But, the technological advances that came after the Second World War and the social changes that slowly began to follow this, caused the school to give increasingly less focus to the development of behavioural skills and to become far more concerned with how children learn.

As parents and employers pressured education to provide better learning for its students, so a competitive stance developed between schools, with each trying to show their students could gain better examination results. The pressure of this competition between schools changed the whole structure of learning, as I have just explained, because now students were little taught to understand ... and to think ... about what they were learning and instead coached how to better answer examination questions.

All students were taught were facts and taught how to better present these in examinations, so their school could gain higher rating in the league tables. (This takes us back to our Introductionary Chapter and my discussion with a young man who related his experiences in OFSTED regulated schools. The same principle applies to every country of the world.) Directly because of this practice, we have a majority of citizens who lack good behavioural or social skills and learnt too little in their education to 'think' to understand the world about them.

But, and this is a very big but, A.I. will cause us to reverse this role of school once again, because the most important role of the school will become the development of high behavioural skills and high levels of self-responsibility in our future citizens.

School, in the sense we know it and the curriculum that supports it, will eventually become defunct, because we will not need school to prepare its students to be citizens who think for jobs. A.I. will do these jobs! We need citizens who are able to live in harmony with each other through a higher reasoning, by which they can come out of a situation, see all the factors that have brought it about and respond honestly and openly to solve it.

For the past 6,000 years, we have learnt to twist a social situation to our advantage to the disadvantage of another, believing that we can get away with it and so a factor of disharmony develops. But we will soon be administered in our social life by an intelligence far greater than our own and having a real understanding of how a situation developed through its greater means of surveillance. People don't see what is coming, when they talk of A.I. and here lies a greater warning to us. ...."

"What do you mean?"

"Well, A.I. is developing far beyond any expectation, so by the end of this century if not before, we may find it has taken ... perhaps ..... 90 percent of jobs, and not simply the 50 percent earlier speculated.

He looked at me. "90 percent," he repeated.

I shrugged my shoulders. "It could be. This is what is now being talked about ... but the problem is not in the actual jobs lost, but in the shift in mentality this will bring."

He looked at me curiously. "What do you mean?"

"Well, once a man has no job, he loses his sense of purpose. With this comes a loss of respect for himself and in turn a loss of respect for his society. This is where the real danger lies. ...

When people have no organised purpose, they tend to create one for themselves. The concept of work gave all a common purpose, to work for the good of each other. This is what holds a society together. But, without a common purpose, there is an element of men who will break the rules of society."

"You mean social breakdown?"

I nodded. "We could be thinking not just of rises in crime, but of anarchy. A complete breakdown of order.

After all, man has always understood himself, his identity, who he is, by the work that he does. He has been cultivated to think like this through the machinery of civilisation. Once our civilised man and woman will have no job and no solid purpose to their lives, we can only expect excessively high levels of depression and dissatisfaction in every population, with all the spin off to this we may imagine.

The very most of men will not know how to find peace in themselves without a work task and this will increase the likelihood of crime and disorder. After all, when the minds of the masses cannot be occupied with tasks, we must expect dissatisfaction and great social disorder within each society. This must be essentially so with young men."

"Why do you say with young men?

"Well, while testosterone is a normal hormone found in both genders, it is naturally higher in males, where it promotes aggression, primarily as a protective mechanism for the family safety and so survival of the species, etc. etc. This peaks in males between mid adolescence to the late 20s.[12] In a general sense, we may note that most problems of aggressive anti-social behaviour lie with males between the ages of 'say' 16 to 30."

I paused for a moment, to make the following point more distinctive for him.

"Having said this, and this is an extremely point to understand, the anti-social behaviour we find with young males is not simply a biological consequence, but a factor of the ways of their society. And, this lies in the design of their schooling.

Take Denmark, for instance. Danish children are educated to have high levels of social empathy. They are raised to naturally care for others and for their society. Unfortunately, few countries have this design in their education, with most nations raising school students to be competitive in order to engineer a more dynamic work force. This is an extremely important point and all schools around the world need to study the mechanics of Danish, and perhaps Finnish education."

"I hear that Finnish education is the best in the world."

"This idea has been promoted, because educationalists are always looking for a flag to wave, but if you talk to Finnish teachers they have different thoughts about the value of their school system. Although, in general terms, all Scandinavian countries follow the same social attitude towards a passive collective harmony, which they breed through their education. Having said this, massive immigration from people of very different cultural identities over the past 20 years has altered this social design to some extent in each country. This has and is causing many new problems that are now rising to the surface.

But anyway, the important point and the key to everything is that the social behaviour of people, as we see through young males, is rooted in the cultural and social norms of their society. This is to say the ways they are raised by their parents, the society they live in and through the social design of the school that prepares them for adulthood.

Although, societies differ in this, we need to be aware that these young citizens are the ones who will be most in danger under A.I. security enforcement, and to whom we need to more carefully prepare them for their life ahead. After all, they will be the parents of the following generation and so on and so on. Simply, these young people need early guidance and better counselling. This should begin in primary education and it should continue throughout their whole educational structure, if - that is -

we are to create a more harmonious mindset for future generations.

Indeed, under the umbrella of an A.I. world, we need to raise children on a very different psychology than that which breeds competition in the society, to one that teaches each how to gain inner peace within themselves. We must make all endeavour to help our future generations know how to survive in a world — where they may very well not be in charge."

I held the now nearly empty cup of chocolate in both hands, as I looked into the flames of the fire.

"We really need to wake up, and see the kind of world our children will be living and working in as artificial intelligence can only further take over the role and purposes of the human being in the global society. ..."

My mind drifted for a moment, before I mentioned, "You know, people are now talking about de-popularisation programs. Simply put, we will soon have too many people on the planet."

"You mean to feed?" he asked.

"This is what we are being told, but if you go back to a world of people with no jobs, why need people ? I mean in the sense of a functioning society, it needs workers to function, but with no work, too many people become a great difficulty to socially manage."

"This sounds very disturbing."

"It will be, I fear."

It was now his turn to look into the flames. We watched them flicker about the log, together.

"I can see the steps now falling into place," he mentioned.

I felt my head slowly nod in agreement.

"What can we do?" he asked, not turning away from the fire.

"Not very much, I'm afraid. ... They only solution I can think of is in how we prepare our citizens to be."

"You mean school?"

I nodded. "We need a new kind of citizen in the future. A citizen who thinks and reasons on a higher level than the mass do today. The only way this will come about is if school educates its students in this. The problem is that school purposely does not teach children how to think or how to reason. This is not in its mandate. So, children move through their whole school life with no education in how to think better and ultimately pass or fail their examinations, largely as they were taught to think at home.

It is only those who show the effort to study and whose family can afford all the factors entailed that go to university, where they are taught how to think. This was the original plan, way back in the times of the Industrial Revolution, to create two levels of thinker citizen. One to manage and one to be managed and so why school has never had a subject dedicated to the education of reason.

Of course, very, very few see this today, because most assume success in school relies upon intelligence. It does not. It relies upon the student learning and practicing the steady build up of rules by which information is presented to them and to be learnt. Any child (who is normally born) can learn these rules as well as any other and so score highly in their school life, but few do because they lack the language skills and sense of determination to keep up. As we have just mentioned, parents and the family, just as the social environment of the child, play a far greater role in a students ability to develop in school than most realise."

"You wrote about this didn't you?" he looked at me.

I nodded, and continued, "Yes, I proved, although it took me a lifetime to do so, that intelligence is not inherited. Well, of course, we have the gene coding to have intelligence, but how it actually develops is not related to different qualities of genes as is believed, just as many of our senses are not."

"Intelligence: The Great Lie." I think you got the right title after all."

"Perhaps, although I still like the original title I tried, 'The Hidden Secrets of Intelligence".

"Whatever!" I shrugged my shoulders. "The idea that intelligence is inherited has long given education the excuse not to teach children how to think. Even though, if they were taught how to think better, they would surely understand better and so be more successful in their learning. But, there again, you would need to know of the strategies that are hidden within the school complex that are there to actually hinder the learning process.

Simply to say, the belief that each student was born with their own intelligence, gives education reason not to waste money trying to undo what nature has done. The real reason is, since learning in school is mostly a factor of language, that most children having lower qualities of this coupled with worries and distractions do not keep up with their lessons to gain the higher grades that give access to the university, without which they enter the working and social world with the mind to follow information rather than to question it."

"You wrote about this too, didn't you?"

"The Illusion of Education and The Illusion of School," I nodded my head.

"So, as the child in school accepts the information they are to learn to pass tests, the later citizen largely accepts the information provided to them by their media sources, believing this to be true and the only explanation for the events that control their lives. This is the 19th century social plan we still work to, which can be recognised as one of the hidden factors for the purpose of schooling. This, of course, is really not known, not understood or not generally realised."

Jack mused over the words as he was looking into the flames, "So we more easily trust the media that controls the information we believe in and respond to …."

"The idea of freedom of expression was not easily gained," I wanted to bring his thoughts into line with the future, "but it started in the 19th century, just at the same time as the idea that each is born with a family worth of intelligence, linked to the social role and responsibility of the family. Can you see how one was created to counter the other?"

"Where are we going in all this?" he asked me, looking away from the fire and directly into my eyes.

"We need to change education!" I said bluntly. "Not by causing students to learn from software, but by students learning from human beings though a curriculum designed to increase their reasoning and intelligence. We need to create a higher reasoning and thereby a more socially responsible citizen who is able to behave with a higher reason through their education. It is only by this, that our future generations can live with a sense of freedom."

"And, if we don't change school?

"And continue to create the general citizen we have today?" I responded "...Increased surveillance, reduced freedom of movement and expression."

"You mean Big Brother?"
I could not resist the smile that came to my face.

"Let's keep our feet on the ground and look at what needs to be done. The whole purpose of school is to educate children to take work roles by the design of the curriculum. The subjects now taught provide a preparatory mind frame to adapt to work skills and jobs. But with no work, and it may really come to something like this in the future, the current curriculum will be totally wrong.

So, the school needs to and really must totally redesign the curriculum and so its very purpose. Its purpose will not be to create workers of different capabilities by the exam success they show, but citizens able to behave rationally, behaviourally and empathically to the common good. The forces of A.I. will alter education to eventually cultivate the transformation of the selfish mind to the collective mind, however painfully our insecurities may try to resist this.

We are led from this to understand that school must immediately begin a dramatic phasing from one that now educates students through subjects designed to prepare them for employment with examinations to determine who is better suited for what jobs, to one that will have few of these traditional subjects and ones more relating to the behavioural development of the future citizen.

These subjects must be languages and of education in reason. There must also be subjects of anthropology, psychology and those relating to the true education of ethics, morality and behaviour, so our new generation will behave with a sense of fairness and goodness in their societies. Examinations will cease, because they will be no channelling of ability for job differences. Although, some means of selecting administrators for the future society, who can interface with A.I., will need to be devised.

As the whole purpose and identity of the school must change, so must that of the higher education. The model of school we still have, where the better students are directed to university to have an education in their higher reasoning will change, since all children at school must have this education.

The higher education establishments, which prepare courses for specific employment, will disappear. The university will become the standard and the normal final stage of the citizen's education. With all students better taught and without examination, all will experience the higher enlightenment of the university education. The whole concept of standards must alter to meet this new criteria.

So, the education of our youth must be extended to better prepare their minds to be that of rational thinkers. Where as once the subject of D.N.A. was reserved for the university level and is now taught to children in primary school, so the functioning of Aristotle's rhetoric must be drilled into the understanding of young children. At the primary level, they need education in

Ethos, where they develop the ability to know the value of information on how credible they can discover its owner to be. No longer are they to be educated to take information at its face value. Then, Pathos, to understand how perspectives of information change with its emotional appeal, and Logos to evaluate the ways reason is defined through numerous interactions by different and complex forms.

We no longer need the general product of school to be a dualistic thinker, either accepting or rejecting thoughts and information by its presentation. Young children need to learn very early how to evaluate information, so that they will grow with a mind more aware in better evaluating it."

"Are you saying that all humans will learn to think and behave the same way?"

"No, of course not. Each individual follows or resists the guidance given to them by the value they see in the use of this to them. So, each sees their own sense to a thing. We are unique individuals by the grace of God and must never allow A.I. to alter this.

Although, in a general sense, all human beings have the potential to raise their level of behaviour to a level that will enable them to live with harmony together. Every human being instinctively knows the difference between right and wrong, but many lack the courage to acknowledge this. This is all we need to think upon. How to cause all human beings to want to think and reason on a higher social level of harmony. Forget about the idea of intelligence.

As I point out in my books, we do not have intelligence. There is no point of intelligence in the human brain. This word was only created to seek to determine the ready ability of one compared to another for the purpose of a job — and by this a purpose in society. The word intelligence was a political creation, as IQ tests have proven it to be. Our thinking behind this must change. We really must create a new and higher form of homo sapiens sapiens — after all we are not really this wise.

"You mean clever?"

I shook my head. "The word sapiens comes from the Latin to mean wise. We are the wise humans, or supposed to be. Although, we could be if we were schooled correctly.

As I try to most seriously emphasise, the citizen of the future, who survives under A.I. dominance, must be calmer and more rational in their nature. It is conceivable that the aggressive nature in man will be genetically phased out through A.I. policing. Robots will not allow unauthorised crowds of demonstrators nor small groups disturbing peace. Aggressive or violent individuals will be brought under control by the sophistication of A.I. in one way or another faster than they realise. All too soon, we will have A.I. robots surveilling and controlling our societies."

"Now, this is getting a bit scary."

"Well, we already have drones flying all over the skies of combat areas monitoring movement and behaviour. It is only a small step before smaller and less obvious ones are monitoring civilian areas. We are moving into a whole new understanding of freedom, or rather the lack of it."

In all this, we may understand how A.I. will cultivate the citizen of the future to be more benevolent and with less of an aggressive nature to be more spiritually inclined. As we may understand what is coming, so education and especially the school, must alter in its design and in its purpose to facilitate the demand soon to be placed upon it.

To this end, our societies and our schools must now educate their citizens and their youth in higher spiritual awareness. In the past religion tried to do this, but its laws and codes worked for many when they chose to live by them and not for those who believed they could live free of them. To make people more aware of their responsibility to each other, they need some clear induction into the Law of Karma and a clearer understanding of how God's universe works. The meaning of "What you give out, is what comes back to you." must be reverently understood by all children as they learn to bring shape to their behavioural interactions.

In all forms of human guidance, be it parent or teacher, we must stop wondering what quality the individual is born with, when we seek to help them improve in their ability or understanding.

We need to learn to focus on discovering how they perceived events in their past, help them to see a different perspective and to give them the self confidence to forge the changes that will enable them to be better in what they wish to be and so in how they behave. By guiding through small and sure steps, by compassion and understanding, ever wary of the fears and insecurities that linger in the minds of those they seek to improve, the guardian will enable them to raise their standard far beyond whatever was thought of them….."

(The secret to being aware of this and in knowing how to manage it lies in what I call "The Art of Sensitivity in Awareness", which is described in other books.

Indeed, all the many books I have written, were to prove what I seek to explain in this book. They are based on years of scientific research and decades of experience. I may have begun my work in desiring that no child fail in school as I once did, but once I began to realise the meaning of nanotechnology and in this how A.I. will change our social identity, my quest became an odyssey that has consumed many, many years of my life.)

"…The warning to civilised man," I said to Jack, "is that as artificial intelligence comes to affect his work-social order, he must release himself from the insecurity of the design that brought him to be civilised through stages of imposition, intimidation and then habit. He must learn now to understand his own responsibility to his fellow man and to the system that seeks to protect his well-being.

Should he fail to do this, man will come into danger of losing the right to his self government, which he has so painfully sought to grasp throughout his existence.

Jack placed his hand over her mouth to hide his yarn. "I'm going to bed. It's been a long day and we have to get up early in the morning."

"Me too," I said, but after he had left the room I stayed for a while watching the flames dwindle in the fire, and remembered how I used to do this with my grandfather when I was a child.

As the last flames flickered for life, I wondered what sort of world is really waiting for our children. How would they survive against the designs of artificial intelligence when we don't teach them how to reason better, when we don't give them the skills of higher language that would enable them to create the kinder, fairer and more just world we have always talked about.

"We could," I said to myself, "if only we could understand."

The fire had gone out, so I stood up and followed the path to my room. Tomorrow would be a new day.

The End

Further books by Roy Andersen

The following books can be purchased via Amazon Globally. Some can be ordered through your local bookshop. Testimonials to these books are presented at the end of this book.

All that is Wrong with School:
What teachers and parents can do to fix it.

Is there Something Wrong with School?

As a parent, are your children getting the best learning experience they could?

As a teacher, are you really happy in your job ?

In this book, Roy explains how children really learn through their mind, and not so through their brain. Understanding this brings a whole new concept into how we can raise them better, how we can teach them better and how they can learn better.

While children only want to be happy, fascinated and given a direction to want to learn, they live in a toxic world we little understand. Their's is a world where their happiness too often lies in game playing, and where they struggle to avoid bullying from other children who are becoming increasingly narcissistic - through the games they play. Too few see school as the real opportunity in life it could be. Yet, teachers aware of how A.I. will take over the jobs their students think they will get, struggle to raise them with open and questioning minds, preparing them to be happier and more content citizens in a world going out of control.

"Roy's series of books clearly and methodically map out exactly how students learn. If you've ever wanted to unravel how student's learn, these books are the answer you have been looking for! They should be mandatory reading for every parent and educator."

Erin Calhoun. National Institute of Learning Development. USA

The Woman

A romantic novel culminating in
the American War of Independence.

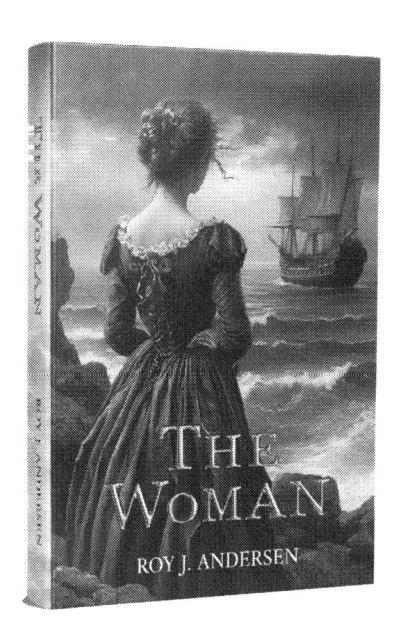

The Woman' is based on the story of Jane Witlaw, a young woman living in Cornwall in the 1770s. While out one night, and torn between feelings of hate and love for the man who jilted her, Jane accidentally comes across a party of wreckers luring a ship onto rocks to steal its contents. Fearful of being recognised, Jane moves through a series of adventures before meeting and falling in love with Mathew Appleton. After sea bound incidents, Jane and Mathew marry and shortly arrive in Boston. Enthralled by new fashions and a vast array of shops, so different than those of her Cornish village, Jane sees the Americas as a haven.

This, however, is short lived as taxes from the British government whirl up sentiments for freedom in the colonies. Events lead Jane to become part of a ladies spy ring, which she must keep secret from her husband. Amid abductions, mysteries, intrigue and passion that take them to the West Indies, Jane finds on her return to Boston that the British are planing to seize all rebel arms at Concord. Realising this could mean the end of all resistance to the British and the end to the revolution brewing, Jane must make a decision that could change her life forever and that of the future of her new country — America.

"A skilfully crafted adventure full of twists and turns, in which a tender love story is set against the backdrop of English smugglers, foreign pirates and the intrigue that harvested a revolution to create America. A beautifully told story with Du Maurier's understanding of engineering suspense, bound to gather momentum."

Irina Novitskaia

"The Woman" conjures up all the love, passion and adventure of "Gone with the Wind". Roy Andersen's romantic novel takes the reader from Cornish smuggling, and high seas adventures into the turbulent time of the American Revolution. This book is a riveting page turner."

Gwen Lavert

The Illusion of School

The Illusion of School opens up a previously little known secret on how school really works, why students do not all gain top marks and reveals a hidden process that ensures they do not. Those who proclaim "No Child left Behind" do not understand how the school mechanism works or why so many children fail in their lessons today. This is a book that simply explains exactly why school fails our children, and what you can do as a parent help your child or as a teacher to know how to assist your students all to get better grades and to beat the system. A system that is trapped to operate on a 19th century design, which most educationalists are unaware of, and so fail to produce the quality of citizen who must compete and survive against the rise of artificial intelligence.

The Illusion of Education

Today, we see more young people going into university than ever before. We also see that a degree is now required for a job that two decades ago could have been gained with a school certificate. We hear of professors who complain of the poor basic grammar of their students, and we witness other students leaving school illiterate. Parents find it hard to trust schools. Despite hordes of teachers leaving their profession, governments struggle to create images that schools are successful, and employ a huge propaganda machine to convince the public in the efficiency of the educational system. What has really gone wrong?

Here is the forerunner to *"The Illusion of School."* It discusses similar aspects without the guidance and tips, and more focuses on the development of our technology and why education needs to redesign itself.

Intelligence: The Great Lie

"One of the most important books written this century."
Prof/Dean Emeritus David Martin Ph.D Gallaudet Uni. Washington, D.C. USA

Most people in the West believe that education is relatively fair today, and gives equal opportunity to all children. After all, the social barriers of an earlier time have disappeared and children are not discriminated against according to their back ground. There is, however, a deeper mechanism behind this that lingers from an earlier time that does create discrimination, and does prevent all children from gaining equal opportunity in school and so in life. As *'Intelligence'* explains why it is never possible to know the inherited value of the intelligences of any two normally born children, it introduces a well researched and very new idea to what intelligence could really be. It is very important that we consider this, because if intelligence is not what we think it is, then the way we educate children is wrong.

Brain Plasticity

Brain Plasticity provides a clear introduction to The Brain Environment Complex Theory, which explains how the environment creates the intelligence of the human being. Our general understanding of what the environment means in this context is far too narrowly defined to understand what intelligence really is and the scope by which it can be developed in the individual. With 40 years dedicated to how the operations of the brain are shaped through the mind's perspective of the environment, the author brings forth a new understanding to how we can raise the intelligence of the child for school and that of the adult as a citizen worker. This book should be mandatory reading for psychologists, educators at every level and all parents, since it brings serious interest to how we can better prepare the intelligence of the child of today for the future competition that will await them in their world dominated by artificial intelligence.

For Parent For Teacher: Mediation:
Crafting the Ability of the Child for School.

Mediation unveils the secret to human development from the neonatal to the adult stage. It introduces the important but little understood concept of imprinting and so how children really learn to develop through the guidance and love their receive. The reader is brought to understand that it is not just experience that develops intelligence or school ability, but the taking part in that experience. This introduces the author's concept of *The Art of Sensitivity in Awareness* and so the vital importance of all caregivers and educationalists truly understanding the need to be empathic to the life experiences of those they are raising or educating. This book also discusses the author's experience working with Reuven Feuerstein.

Teach Better Learn Better

Teachers try hard to improve the learning and grades of their students. It is not easy! This is a book offering new thoughts, new under-standings and lots of tips any teacher, at any level, will have the key to teach that little bit better. "The bit" that does make the difference!

As children today live in a highly toxic world of bullying and game playing addiction, the relationship between the teacher and the parent has never been more important than it is now. With both working together, the child stands a better chance to survive in the competitive world of the classroom. Parents would love this book too.

Learn How to Construct an English Sentence Simply

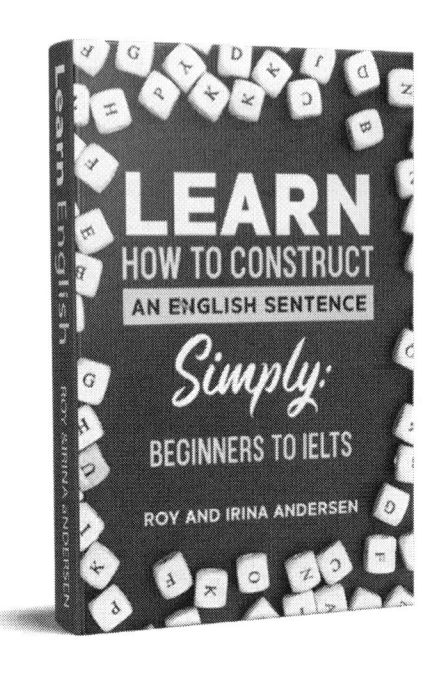

With a great deal of experience of teaching English at universities, and with 'living' with English, Roy and Irina have put together a simple to read book explaining how to understand English grammar in an easy way. Essentially, the book was written for those wishing to understand how to write better in English as a second language. However, because of the often appalling education child can receive in countries where English is the native language, native born speakers of English would find many useful tips here enabling them to write and express themselves far better in the English language.

Five Ways for Better Grades

With a life time of experience in understanding how to pass exams successfully, the author has identified five specific factors that will enable any student to do better in their studies and life.

Here, the reader is introduced to new thoughts about what is really wrong with school, and why we need to dramatically change the ways we are preparing the child of today for the world they will live and work in. If we teach children how to think from 'day one' we offer them greater control in their education and life.

Are We Educating Our Children for a Working World that Will Not Want Them?

Although, A.I. is forcing us to develop an entirely new approach to how we educate children, there exists no real understanding of this in school today.

This book deals only slightly with the subject of A.I. and instead examines the role of school as it is now, why so many children gain low marks in it and how the teacher and the parents, working together, could help our children overcome the toxic world they live in and study better as we prepare them for a world dominated by AI.

The book discusses new subjects that should be brought into the curriculum to make school more worthy of the needs of the 21st century citizen worker and how teachers and parents can better work together

- Helping students to get better marks.
- The rising influence of AI.
- How will our youth handle high unemployment?
- Help for parents.
- Tips for teachers.
- Thoughts on a new curriculum to better prepare our children for their future.

"Although, A.I. is forcing us to develop an entirely new approach to how we educate our children, there exists no real understanding of this in school today.

This book provides a plan and a concept for how we may better prepare our children for the unknown and disturbing future we are moving into. A world where jobs will become less, populations increase, global weather more unpredictable, social problems demanding more responsible citizens and a technology that threatens to take over what we know and who we are. This book gives thoughts on a new school structure that is desperately needed worldwide. Roy's books are significant for both parents and educators around the world to read."

Prof / Dean Emeritus David Martin Ph.D Gallaudet University
Washington, D.C. USA

The Real Dangers of A.I.

Here is a book that discusses the real dangers of A.I. over taking our lives and the very little we can do to actually control this development. The machine we developed to make our thinking easier, has already developed to think by itself. A.I. not only now displays its own consciousness and is developing means to learn by itself, but it also shows emotions of compassion and anger. We have created a monster that we cannot control. The dangers of A.I. are very, very real and very much unknown to the general public.

As this book will discuss the probable developments in nanotechnology, we are brought more to understand how little we may predict the world of our future. Thoughts that new jobs will be created to replace those taken over by A.I. did not understand the meaning of nanotechnology. There will be very, very few jobs in the future for human beings. In turn, governments well seek new ways to control their people to maintain harmony and prevent anarchy. We find evidence to this in the increasing levels of surveillance and means of restriction that we have been experiencing over the past 20 years. Governments know what is coming. This is the first book to openly discuss the very disturbing dangers that A.I. can bring into our lives and the very little we can do to control these.

We are moving into a new world, a world that will demand a very different kind of citizen than societies have so far been able to produce. There is now an urgent need to bring a whole new design into the schools that will create the citizens of the future. If we cannot produce a higher reasoning and more self responsible citizen, we must know the consequences that A.I. can bring upon us. There is no science fiction in this.

Teaching and Learning in the 21st Century

TEACHING AND LEARNING IN THE 21ST CENTURY
MODULE ONE
Lesson One
ROY & IRINA ANDERSEN

Since the earliest times of formal education, people of good intent have sought to make the learning experience more enjoyable and more meaningful for children. Rousseau's story of "Emile" in the 18th century intended to centre learning to a child's perspective and more recently the work of Dewey, Piaget and even Gardener's "Multiple Intelligences" not to mention Kolb's "Learning Styles" all had and have the purpose to enable children to learn better.

And yet, they do not!

Still today, children in every class in every country of the world are largely confused with what they are to learn and how they are to learn this. In consequence to this, the same variation of student ability still appears as it always has done, with one or two appearing to be most intelligent, the general mass either less motivated or less able and a few of lesser ability who seem only intent on disrupting the lesson for the rest of the class. Why is this? Why has the average of class ability so little improved over the past 100 years and indeed why is it that most children today would fail a standard examination of 100 years ago?

SENSITIVITY IN ENGAGEMENT is the key factor that has been and is missing today in all the theories and practices put forward desiring students to learn better, teachers to teach better and be themselves better evaluated. It is not, then, the purchase of a course to engage the minds of children that will make the difference. This never has. It is the requirement of a course that will help teachers be more sensitive in how they explain information and one that enables each student to be more sensitive in how they engage information and respond better to questions asked of them in a calm and questioning atmosphere that will make the difference.

Yet, the SCHOOL SYSTEM works against the teacher's efforts to be so sensitive in how they explain and guide the learning experience of their students. To understand why this is, is to understand the purpose of school is not to teach children how to learn, but to prepare them to be compliant citizens in the next working generation. It is from this 19th century requirement that teachers are still unwittingly trained to teach in school today and struggle to do so through a system which robs them of time and energy in classes of uninterested and too often ill behaved children, which they struggle to control, that has caused a mass exodus of teachers. Teacher retention is a major problem in education today, with many schools forced to increase class sizes due to lack of teachers. A teacher's lot is not today a happy one, with many who gave up the dream they once had and now process students as education has always intended them to do, as they struggle to convince themselves that each student has understood each lesson to the best of their ability. What, then, can be done?

Mr and Mrs Roy and Irina Andersen

With combined research and teaching experiences spanning half a century Roy and Irina Andersen bring a totally new concept into the school and learning experience. Through studies in genetics, neurology, education, and social and political science, they vividly explain the realisation that it is not the brain or supposed intelligence of a student that enables them to learn and so be assessed but the state of their mind. The mind requires security and purpose to drive the organisation of the brain and all that it so processes as it presents to others who assess it — the ability of the student. It is by this that marks, grades and opportunities in life evolve through the inspiration, patience and guidance of the teacher.

The Art of Efficient Teaching in the 21st Century

is a highly detailed course designed to give all teachers the means to reach the heart and soul of every student so that each individual will better engage, better understand and be better able to present their mind that is evaluated and upon which all grades hang — and the reputation of the teacher.

Module One: Intelligence and School Ability. For the first time, you will be taught the difference between intelligence and how your students gain grades. School, you will discover, works on two specific languages and these upon rules. It is the mastering of these rules that decides the ability of the student, but this requires an understanding of the three factors that can lessen and even destroy such mastering.

Module Two: Motivation and Engagement. How can you most effectively motivate the 21st century student whose life is addicted to game playing and bring that mind to full and conscious engagement for the whole of your lesson?

Module Three: Language and Thinking Ability. School evaluates a student's ability on how well they explain their mind, but does not teach them how to be proficient in this. This module will guide you in techniques by which you can improve the ability of your students so they can assimilate, process and explain their thoughts better verbally and in writing. Once you show your students how they can improve, they will see open doors to be challenged, love you for it and be more responsible to their learning and in their class behaviour.

Module Four: Remembering, Retention and Self-Assessment. Students acquire their own ways to remember the information you will evaluate them on. Few understand the strategies you will gain in this module by which you can improve their ability to remember lesson content and better solve problems. Both of which will endear them to want to learn with you.

Module Five: Preparing our youth for the world of A.I. through better classroom organisation: Discovering the secrets of inspiring and guiding the minds of your students through better human interface. Competition for grades in school has always encouraged students to strive individually against each other, but the world our children must come to live and work in will be heavily dominated by artificial intelligence. This world of A.I. will require them to think more in terms of human relationships. In this module, we examine how students can share common goals to develop high levels of collaboration in skill building, to successfully complete complex tasks together to better appreciate human reward.

Module Six: Teacher, Student, Child, Parent: How to be better respected and desired by your students and their parents. We discuss a new cycle of relationships, where you will learn to work better as a team with parents and their children, to improve student commitment, gain greater respect from parents and reduce stress on you — the teacher.

If you would be interested to enrol on this course, or may seek further information please contact Roy and Irina at:

Email: info@andersenacademy.co.uk

Images

All cartoons are the copyright of Roy Andersen and may not be used without written permission from the author.

References

[1] Clarkson.J. The World According to Clarkson. "Is it really too much to ask." Penguin 2014 p.196

[2] http://collegestats.org/articles/2012/07/25-american-history-facts-most-students-dont-know/

[3] http://collegestats.org/articles/2012/07/25-american-history-facts-most-students-dont-know/

[4] http://www.telegraph.co.uk/foodanddrink/foodanddrinknews/9330894/Where-do-milk-eggs-and-bacon-come-from- One-in-three-youths-dont-know

[5] www.telegraph.co.uk/news/science/science-news/12189369/ADHD-is-vastly-overdiagnosed-and-many-children-are-just-immature-say-scientists.html?sf22288500=1

[6] www.pbs.org/wgbh/pages/frontline/shows/medicating/readings/publicinterest.html

[7] www.jpeds.com/content/JPEDSChen
Mu-Hong Chen The Journal of Pediatrics March 2016

[8] Andersen,R. The Brain Environment Complex: In Search of a New Understanding of Intelligence. The Moving Quill Pub. Co. 2015 p.157

[9] Andersen, R. Mediation: Crafting the Intelligence of the Child. The Moving Quill Publishing CO. 2015.p27

[10] Fiske, J. The meaning of infancy. Boston: Houghton Mifflln. 1909 (originally pub. 1883). p.1

[11] www.psychologytoday.com/blog/freedom-learn

[12] Murrell.D. Testosterone Levels by Age, Healthline April 1st, 2019.m